PARENTING
IN THE AGE OF
ANXIETY

Dr Zirak Marker is a renowned child and adult psychiatrist and psychotherapist with clinical training at the Westchester Medical Centre, New York University. He has been practising for fifteen years in the space of education psychology, guiding students with learning disabilities, developmental delays, and autism. He is currently the CEO (chief executive officer) of the Aditya Birla Integrated School for children with different learning needs.

Dr Marker consults for various schools in Mumbai, and at the Saifee Hospital. He has conducted innumerable workshops and given lectures to students, teachers, parents, and other professionals. For his outstanding contribution to children with learning disabilities, Dr Marker has been felicitated by the Mancherji Edalji Joshi Memorial Trust, and for his contribution to education, he has been awarded by the Zoroastrian Trust Funds of India.

PARENTING IN THE AGE OF ANXIETY

ANXIETY

Raising the Careworn Generation

DR ZIRAK MARKER

RUPA

Published by
Rupa Publications India Pvt. Ltd 2016
7/16, Ansari Road, Daryaganj
New Delhi 110002

Sales centres:
Allahabad Bengaluru Chennai
Hyderabad Jaipur Kathmandu
Kolkata Mumbai

ISBN: 978-81-291-3774-6

10 9 8 7 6 5 4 3 2 1

First impression 2016

The moral right of the author has been asserted.

Typeset by SÜRYA, New Delhi
Printed in India at Nutech Print Services, Faridabad

CONTENTS

CONTENTS

FOREWORD

Dr Zirak Marker, in his inimitable style, has penned an absolute must-read book for all parents. *Parenting in the Age of Anxiety*— a new age parenting Bible—covers topics that parents and children grapple with on a daily basis and issues that are very challenging to understand.

Dr Marker has logically explained the 'whys' surrounding complex subjects such as stress and anxiety, and throws light on 'how' to handle them very simply, while keeping the emotional wellbeing of the child as the primary focus. The book aims to empower helpless and guilt-ridden parents, who struggle to resolve or make sense of what's happening to their child. Equally, it hopes to tear down the stigma associated with several developmental issues that confront children.

Written in a manner that is very simple to understand, this book can potentially alter lives and bring about a positive change across families and homes.

Neerja Birla
Mumbai, 2016

INTRODUCTION

The Birth of Anxiety

*'It is vital that while educating our children's brains...
we do not neglect to educate their hearts...'*
—Dalai Lama

Perhaps one of the hardest things I have done was to write about myself, yet I needed to, and it has been part of my journey in life. Writing for me has always been cathartic and introspective. I can express myself and my feelings best through writing. I then can reflect on matters and get better perspective and clarity of thought. Most importantly, I have not buried or suppressed issues deep within my being. Writing has been a wonderful tool for my work as well. I have encouraged many parents and children, husbands, and wives to write to themselves, each other or me. Some prefer handwritten notes, messages or old-fashioned letters. Some prefer messaging on their cell phones or using emails. Whichever way or medium it is, it's the expression of your feelings and emotions that is vital. It helps to sift thoughts or issues that are not important enough for you to share from those that are. It lets you realize the significance of your own thoughts, issues or state of mind in the present, of what you need to express to a loved one. It helps in letting go...

My journey with anxiety began when I was about twelve years old. I was in class seven. When I returned home from school one day, my parents sat with my brother and me to have a talk. Within minutes they told us that my mother had a lump in her breast, which had to be surgically removed the following day at Breach Candy hospital; until she recovered in a couple of days we would stay with my grandmother.

I remember my fingers turning numb. Cold sweat spread through my entire body. I felt I was choking, my mouth went dry and I could hear my heart exploding within my chest. My vision was blurring and I wanted to throw up but could not. I wanted to ask a hundred questions but did not. I wanted to cry but dared not. A lump meant cancer, the dreaded word we all had heard about. An illness which often had no cure. An illness which meant long-term suffering, painful treatment, needles, surgery, and death. I think I must have had my first panic attack then. My world had collapsed.

What if Mom died? What if she never came back from the hospital? What if the treatment didn't work? How would Dad look after us or do all the things that Mom did? Shouldn't I tell her how much we love her? Why was God so cruel to give her this disease when she was only forty-two years old? I stopped believing in God right then.

My mother went through an entire year or so of intensive chemotherapy and radiation—and survived. She was a fighter. She never gave up. However, cancer had taken its toll on all of us emotionally and psychologically, in different ways.

I internalized my distress and stopped communicating. I became withdrawn and quiet. I thought I should not complain or burden my parents with any of my problems after what Mom had been through. I suddenly became, or tried to become, more independent. I studied harder and did better in my exams. I think I grew up overnight. But the next three years of my life became living hell. I shared this trauma with my loved ones only in the years to come.

Perhaps because of the situation at home and staying isolated in school as a coping mechanism, I became a target for bullying and comments. I became the class 'loser' with no friends (by then I was ostracized by my own group of friends as no one would talk to me). I was called names like 'nerd' and 'pansy'—I didn't even know the meanings of some of those names. I became an embarrassment. I was even spat on. I was never invited for any cool parties, events or birthdays. I wasn't allowed to play with anyone, or to stand or sit in places the 'cool kids' would use. If I touched another child's desk in class by mistake, I was abused by my classmates, who would wipe down the part that I had touched saying that I had 'polluted' it. Random boys would whack me hard on my back and run off. I wouldn't even know who. I was told by my ex-friends that I was so pathetic and ugly that I should die. Sadly, I believed them all. I would sometimes hide in the stinking bathroom or sit in the library all through the lunch break to avoid being hurt. I once stood on the balcony outside the art room in school contemplating whether I should jump to end my miserable life. I would sometimes break down in school itself and everyone would laugh even harder. I would cry myself to sleep most nights. I was suffering alone in silence. There was not a soul to speak to or share my feelings with at school. When I came back home, it was to a silent house as Mom was usually in the hospital for her chemotherapy cycles. I was anxious, fearful and depressed all the time. I stopped eating, lost weight and fell sick many times. I started hating those boys and girls in school with all my heart. I dreaded waking up each morning, going in for a shower and getting into that school uniform which I grew to hate. I wanted revenge. I wanted to fight. I wanted justice. I wanted to stand up for my basic rights, for this cruelty to stop. But my spirit was so broken that I didn't even know how to fight back or whom to turn to. I tried talking to a few children, begged them to stop. I kept asking them why they behaved as they did, asked to be forgiven, but never received any answers and until today, I still don't know why this ever happened to me. I craved company, conversation, friendship or just niceness from anyone.

I was by then riddled with complexes, low self-esteem, and no confidence. Finding it difficult to maintain prolonged eye contact or hold a conversation, I developed tics and peculiar habits. I began biting the inside of my mouth, which later led to ulcers. I forgot how to express myself or share my feelings. I had lost my creativity, drive or motivation to strive, to aim at goals. I had become cold, cynical, irritable, depressed, and mechanical. I had given up…almost.

The only creature who gave me comfort, unconditional love, and distracted me for hours through the week, and put millions of smiles on my face was my dog, Gucci. He was everything to me at that time. He knew. And he could comfort me in ways that maybe no human could, in those moments of grief and darkness. He could sense my loneliness in his own superior way. He would sit close to me, so I could cuddle him for security, and sleep peacefully on many difficult nights. God bless his soul.

But then, my school days were over and I joined junior college, which changed me. Students there actually accepted and loved me for who I was and thus I gave myself another chance. I made some of my closest and dearest friends there, who are still like family to me today. I believed in myself once again. I held on to those friendships with all my heart. I was laughing and smiling again. Life became beautiful. I discovered my strengths and worked on my weaknesses. I tried to become more positive. At this point I started becoming more and more intrigued with human attitudes and behaviour. I wanted to understand human beings in more depth. I wanted to learn about different personalities. In some way, I subconsciously needed answers, to heal myself. I needed to understand and forgive, so that I could let go of my past and move on in my life without baggage.

After medical school, I was very clear that I wanted to pursue psychology and psychiatry. I wanted to learn more so I could be well equipped to help children going through similar problems. I did not realize that this desire to help others would then become my life's passion and work. However, over the years, anxiety has remained close to me in numerous ways. It has never really gone. It comes, sometimes most unexpectedly, but then there are long stretches of time when I am free from these moments of panic. Sometimes the slightest provocation or minimal stress can cause its reappearance. When the symptoms surface, many memories and apprehensions do come back, although very faintly. But I do know that my past experiences have left a scar, one that may never really go away. But it's an imprint of what I have learned, what I used to be, and how the world needs to be.

Today, I am married to an amazing woman and I'm the father of two beautiful children, a boy and a girl. Until then I did not know what parental love was or how it was meant to feel. I never thought I had it in me to love so much, when I sometimes felt my heart would explode (and not, thankfully, because of a panic attack!). I am not perfect and constantly still searching for answers, to explore myself within, to know who I am. I am neither a perfect person nor a perfect parent, but want to make changes so that people may become nicer and gentler. I want a world for my children devoid of hatred, for them to be tolerant and accepting. I want them to always be and feel safe. I want to constantly keep learning and be the catalyst of the change that I want to see in my children. I hope this little book, filled with notes, insights and writings help you, the reader, to change, especially if you want to be a parent in today's world and ensure that your child always remains happy.

The Birth of Anxiety

Every child experiences some kind of anxiety through growing years. This is normal. Right from the time of conception there is an element of stress, concern, worry or anxiety in a child's life.

Is this anxiety transferred by us as parents to our newborn? Every new parent has sleepless nights thinking about all sorts of hazards or possibilities. As parents, we have a dream-child concept. We imagine how our babies will look when they're born, how perfectly they will behave or how intelligent they may become. We dream that they will be these little angels with amazing sleeping or eating patterns, no tantrums, going through smooth transitions in different phases of their early months. We dream about their academic achievements and how proud they're going to make us feel. We even imagine what kind of personalities they should possess and who they should become.

Most of this changes when babies are born! We, as new parents leap off our beds at night to check if our newborn is still breathing or not. Our vigilance, alertness and paranoia become ten-fold. Has any dangerous object gone into our children's mouths or nostrils by mistake? Has the pillow smothered them? Will they roll off the bed; choke or aspirate? Are they progressing through their normal developmental milestones and are they growing healthy, getting enough nutrition? Have bottles been sterilized properly? Are the nannies or nurses we have hired, treating our babies with enough care or are they negligent and rough when not watched? Are the children going to get admission or settle well in play groups and nursery schools? Are they going to grasp concepts and learn as quickly or easily as other kids in their class? Or are they going to be bullied in school, going to get their hearts broken…?

Added to these thoughts are endless diaper changes, sleepless nights and feeding rituals. In fact, a stressed-out, overanxious or hyper parent will more likely have a difficult child with challenging behaviour.

The discovery of human mirror neurons in the brain has raised much debate and enthusiasm in the neuroscientific community. Evidence from functional magnetic resonance imaging (FMRI) has shown that the exact same brain regions become active both when an action is being performed and observed. Indeed, in the early 1900s, Italian researchers—who had implanted electrodes in the brains of several macaque monkeys to study the animals' brain activity—found that the neurons in the monkeys' premotor cortex began firing not only when the monkeys reached out for their own food, but also if they happened to watch a hungry researcher eat his lunch! In our everyday life therefore, we recoil if someone trips; we yawn if the person next to us does; or we smile if the baby we hold chortles.

The human mirror neuron system has helped us understand, more profoundly, numerous subjects such as action, intention, understanding, imitation, language, empathy, and self-awareness. It has helped us come to grips with role modelling and the imprinting of behaviours.

Thus, could the perception or display of anxieties or fears in children be a mirroring of our own fears and anxieties as caregivers? Does this culminate into learned behaviour? Do our children learn from us how to feel anxious, nervous or afraid at some subconscious level? Do our apprehensions transfer onto them? How much of it is nature, temperament, and genetics versus nurture, upbringing, and environment? Is all this essentially the dysregulation of neurotransmitters in the brain?

Anxiety is also a natural human response to a perceived danger or threat. It is a biological and neuro-physiological function, called the fight—flight response, when stress hormones are released to prepare the body to safeguard itself.

It is natural for unfamiliar or difficult situations to initiate feelings of anxiety, nervousness or uneasiness in children. Stress can manifest at a very young age in the form of stranger anxiety, separation anxiety or social anxiety. Apprehensions or fears about anything 'unknown' leads to anxiety. There could be endless triggering factors. It may be the child's first day in school, birth of a sibling, parent returning to a job, daycare centres, fear of certain people or situations, a movie or a particular character in a show, intolerance of certain sounds, smells, places, visual stimuli, textures, unpleasant situations with a peer or friend; or news about wars, terrorism, global warming, natural calamities, and disasters.

Then there are more significant factors that lay the seed of anxiety in children, such as the loss or death of a loved one or parent, parental disharmony, parents' divorce, abuse, major life transitions, moving to a new city or school, medical problems or disability.

Signs to Look Out For in Children

- Excessive worry or nervousness on most days of the week for a protracted period.
- Disturbed sleep at night or sleepiness through the day.
- Irritability, moodiness and difficulty in concentrating (always appearing preoccupied), which affects daily functioning.
- Negative and pessimistic attitude, always thinking the worst could happen.

- Feeling a sense of dread and impending doom, as if something bad is going to happen.
- Psychosomatic and physical symptoms such as headaches, stomach aches, muscle tension, feeling unwell, tiredness and fatigue, dizziness, chest pains, nausea, tingling, numbness or cold sweats.
- Refusal to go to school and social avoidance.
- Panic attacks, with a sudden onset of physical symptoms that can include palpitations in the chest, shortness of breath, a choking sensation, dizziness, blurring of vision, feeling faint, and stomach discomfort.

What We Need to Do

Accept that there is a problem and do not attribute the symptoms to the child's personality or temperament.

Many parents feel that pushing their kids and being tougher with them would help them overcome their anxieties and become stronger. This does not work as the child will only start internalizing his or her feelings, resulting in a breakdown of communication.

Be supportive, caring, understanding and non-judgmental, while trying to understand what children are really feeling and what the triggering factors for the onset of anxiety may be.

Get a feedback from the child's environment areas—school teachers, friends, coaches, and helpers so you can identify troublespots.

Use identification as a process, by talking about and sharing your own fears or anxieties first, so that the child doesn't feel alone and can relate better to you when he/she needs to. Also talk to him/her about strategies that you may have used to generate solutions and overcome certain problems.

Depending on the child's age, a rational explanation about

the physiological aspects of anxiety and the pre-emption of it sometimes helps.

Seeking professional guidance and counselling for both the parent and child are very crucial, so that certain aspects are not missed. Medication may also be required sometimes.

Let your child know that you are there for him/her, no matter what, and help come up with a solution together. Try to solve problems by making an effort to address them. Think of different combinations and permutations, urge the child to think and allow him/her to feel that an independent decision or solution has been reached.

Rationalizing certain situations with maturity is also important. A child needs to know that everybody in life has problems, worries, and concerns.

Introspect and curtail some of your own reactions to stress, fears, situations or problems to be a more effective role model and problem-solver. Be optimistic, calm and in control so that further strength and balance are achieved.

*

There are always two paths leading to opposite destinations. One leads us to regret, bitterness, and pain; the other takes us to happiness, forgiveness, and peace.

I chose the latter. I chose to use my experiences to heal myself, thereby healing others in pain, helping families overcome bitterness and replace it with happiness. To punish others or inflict pain to feel a sense of vindication, to become cynical, vengeful, hateful and unforgiving only lead to frustration and unhappiness. Pushing loved ones away and withdrawing will result in a sense of being terribly lonely.

I chose the other path. I chose to learn. That gave me deeper understanding and provided me with answers. I began to understand myself better. It made the pain go away and memories fade. It made me stronger as I empowered myself to become a better human being. I always believed in goodness and the power of being a 'nice' human being. I chose to forgive and let go. What was most healing though, was the strength, sensitivity and empathy I found within myself to help and guide others, the sense of immense and deep fulfilment when I could lead another person or family to peace, happiness, and healing. A chance to introspect, make changes and make things right within themselves first. But what I learned through this journey most importantly, is that everybody in life has a choice to make, a path to choose, a journey to take. A choice to be happy, a choice to change and be the parent of an amazing young child who will then take these choices forward in his/her own lifetime to find his/her rightful place in this world…

Chapter 1

UNREAL EXPECTATIONS

Academic Stress and Pressures

*'This is the very perfection of a man, to find out
his own imperfections.'*
—St Augustine

To
Ms Menezes,
The Principal
Edushare School

Dear Ma'am,

*I write to you as I have the highest regard for you and
know that you can bring about change. Both my children,
Ahaan and Ishaan, were under your guidance and care for
many years. Ahaan is doing wonderfully well for himself
and is working with a prestigious firm in Singapore. He was
always a high ranker at your school, being in the top five for
years. He was known to all his teachers and faculty members
for being very methodical, bright, and diligent. I think that
was also one of the reasons why he was chosen to be the
headboy, which really boosted his self-confidence, made him
believe in himself further and maximize his potential. For
all of that I am ever grateful to you and the school teachers.
My son has been moulded and nurtured well by each of you
at school. However, in saying that I know it was easy for all
of you as it was for me, because of his innate intellect. His
personality and hard work combined to make him
academically successful. Even now, he is extremely goal-*

oriented and focused. He has already chalked out his five-year plan and has been independent for a few years.

My letter to you, however, is regarding Ishaan. From as far back as I can remember, he was known as 'Ahaan's brother' at Edushare. That label was the beginning of many others that would follow, this perhaps being the most damaging. After he came into class six, I was called into school almost every term. The minute a letter or note in his diary arrived home, I would get nervous and my heart would pound with anxiety. Those nights before meetings with teachers would be disturbed for me. Most teachers would always say the same thing over and over again.

'Mrs Thakker, Ahaan's brother is almost as bright as him, but he is not studying hard enough. He daydreams in class and keeps looking out of the window. He has so much potential but it does not reflect in his examination papers. He writes answers in his own words and elaborates too much. Sometimes his imagination gets the better of him and his descriptive answers are too long. He has to learn to answer to the point and use textbook language. Some of the words and vocabulary he uses are too fanciful. Examiners may not understand his language. Even when he gets his marks (always in the range of 60–70 per cent), he seems okay with them. He also asks too many questions in class, which can get distracting for others. Please see that he studies more at home, copies and writes his answers for practice two or three times on a ruled sheet of paper…'

The suggestions were endless and futile.

How could I tell them that these suggestions were irrelevant? What was asked of him was contrary to his nature and abilities. Ishaan was and is a dreamer. He has a mind of his own and is an independent thinker. He hated studying, especially if he had to rote-learn definitions or long answers. He hated writing or copying down answers on a piece of paper as he thought it was not practice but a waste of time. He loved literature and devoured two to three books or novels in a week. They were mostly not age-appropriate, but he never enjoyed books written for children. He was not a conformist and disliked being told how to do things repeatedly. He loved nature and animals, music and poetry, writing and travelling. He thought that our educational system was like a strait-jacket and marks and examinations made no sense. Everything taught was exam-oriented, tailored from the point of view of questions expected in an examination.

How could I tell these teachers that they needed to recognize his strength and potential and not keep focusing on what he needed to improve on? He was never appreciated for his long answers in literature or his eloquent essays. He was pulled up for not paying attention and when he asked questions, he was told that he was disturbing the class. He felt he was always being compared to his brother at school and was never understood by his teachers. The turning point, unfortunately, was in class nine, when I started believing what his teachers were saying. That is when Ishaan shut down and did not care to study or push himself beyond a point. I had finally succumbed to the pressure and Ishaan was affected by my stress. I do not know whether to blame myself, the other mothers of his peers, the school or the educational system.

I forced him to take private tuitions in almost all subjects. Towards the middle of class ten he had as many as twenty hours of tuitions each week. I dissuaded him from reading novels and almost threw one out from our window after an altercation with him over studies. I had become a 'helicopter mom' and started hovering outside his bedroom, spying on him to see how much he was actually studying. I would scream at him if I did not find him at his study table. I had pulled him out of his twice-a-week athletic programme and he never found time to swim at the club, which he loved to do thrice a week, irrespective of his crazy schedules. I removed the cable TV from his bedroom and we fought daily over his Facebook and screen time or mobile phone usage. My husband and I used to fight as I refused to believe that I was doing anything wrong. He kept telling me to leave our son alone and I could not. I had been sucked into this force which I believed was in the best interest of my child. It had to be right as every parent was apparently doing the same thing, every child had the same number of classes and tuitions, and was studying harder than my son.

All through these painful months, Ishaan started resenting me. I would often hear him mutter angrily when I snatched his mobile phone away. I would be up at nights worrying about Ishaan. What would the school and his teachers think if he did not perform? Which college would give him admission if he did not get 90 per cent? Students nowadays were scoring even 98 and 99 per cent! What would others think of me as a mother? I had allowed myself to get sucked into that black, never-ending, deep hole of pressure, and the irrational expectations and assumptions of what a perfect child should be.

Looking back, I cannot even understand why I felt so pressurized. I knew that my son was intelligent in a non-conventional way. Earlier, I used to actually make fun of the other so-called paranoid or hyper moms in his class. I would disregard some of the negative feedback of the class teachers. I would make a very conscious and concerted effort not to compare my two children. Yet, there came a time when, in anger, I would tell Ishaan to see how motivated Ahaan was, how dedicated to his studies and career. The home environment then became extremely negative and stressful. Ishaan and I hardly spoke about anything except his studies and exams.

We went through four long, hard years like this. Eventually, he got brilliant marks, topping both in class ten as well as class twelve. Parents envied me and I thought I had done the best thing for my son. I was proud of myself and sometimes mocked my husband for believing otherwise.

A few nights after Ishaan's last board examination paper, he must have stayed up late while reading his novel and had fallen asleep, book on chest and reading lamp left on. When I woke up to use the bathroom, I noticed the light and went into his bedroom to switch it off and cover him up. While I was pulling up his blanket, I noticed something very odd. There were patches on his forearms where his hair was missing. When I bent down and pushed up his pyjamas, I found the same on his legs and when I kissed his forehead, I found three significant bald patches on his scalp as well. This worried me and we took Ishaan to our family doctor the next day.

He was diagnosed with 'trichotillomania' or hair-pulling disorder which is a psychological, compulsive urge to pull out one's hair, which can go on for weeks and months. It is mainly caused by high levels of stress and pressure on children or young adults. Severe anxiety causes it, resulting in considerable guilt, shame, and low self-esteem. I felt I was the worst mother in the entire universe. How could I ever forgive myself for causing so much stress to Ishaan? I had to change the situation. I had to find a solution and reverse matters. I had to find answers.

Today, my Ishaan has set up and heads an online educational system for non-conventional learners and students who have learning disabilities. He has a team of eighty people working under him. He has received three international young entrepreneurs' awards already at the age of twenty-nine. He helps over two hundred schools and educational institutes and has touched the lives of hundreds of students, making a difference. He has brought about a 'change'!

He left for the US shortly after college in India and pursued further studies in child and educational psychology. There was no looking back. He keeps promising to come back, but I do not think he has forgiven me. I do not think he will return. I am so proud of him, but I do not have the courage or strength to say those words to him.

Thus Ms Menezes, I urge you to bring about a change in your school and initiate a different approach to students. I urge you to mould the mindsets of the teachers. I only write this to you, so that other parents may not take the path that I wrongly chose.

I thank you once again for all that you have done for my two sons.

Yours sincerely,
Mrs Thakker

Psychology of Perfectionist Parenting

We all want the best for our child. However, we do not realize that, slowly, it becomes wanting perfection from him/her. Perfectionism can turn parenting stressful not just for the child but the entire family. Having irrational expectations and making unrealistic demands come from parental insecurities. Parents seem to measure their own success by the achievements of their children, sometimes feeling that this would mask their own inadequacies and weaknesses. When this happens, parents become more aggressive, authoritative, and irrational. They begin controlling the child and become over-dominating.

This creates extreme stress and anxiety in children. They

become over-dependent on their controlling parent to a point where their thinking capabilities and decision-making skills get compromised. They are riddled with complexes, low self-confidence, and poor self-esteem. They start linking being loved with their own attainment (or not) of perfection. This further worsens fears and anxieties, making them feel very low and rejected if they cannot cope or live up to parental expectations. They become so unsure of their parents that the smallest of mistakes for them are big issues. They constantly worry that they will disappoint them or let them down. Such children play less, become quiet, socially awkward or withdrawn, and become less creative. They get frustrated with routine academic work and cannot deal with studies when the level of difficulty increases. They develop unhealthy coping mechanisms. For example, some children get extremely slow at their work and keep obsessively rubbing out their written work until it is perfect. Others lose the motivation to develop their own strengths and talents. Learning and retention may also become difficult for these children in classrooms.

Many children become perfectionists themselves as they continuously feel the pressing need to please their parents. In the process, they lose their personal identities and do not recognize who they truly are. Children then are more likely to experience symptoms of depression or sometimes even Obsessive Compulsive Disorder (OCD)—an anxiety disorder in which repetitive thoughts and behaviour occur, leading to a pressing need to perform rituals or repetitive routines, such as constant washing of hands. Children start avoidance behaviours, refusing to face any challenges. They do not know how to assume or accept responsibility. They do not want to take risks as they fear failure. Some children may even start manifesting behavioural problems or rebellious conduct. Severe sibling rivalry is also common when parents tend to compare children.

Unfortunately, if there is no rectification or change in parenting styles, these children will grow up to have problems through most of their young adult lives, affecting their career paths and relationships. As a consequence, they may become such parents themselves, which could harm yet another generation.

Insights for Parents

Your child's achievements, performances or failures are not a reflection of the kind of parent that you are, or your capabilities. Perfection itself is a perception and a concept. Thus, we can thus never perfectly perceive anything. We only know that the search for perfection is a 'process'.

Accept and understand that your child has innate, inborn potential, talents, and strengths that need to be explored and honed, without constantly giving importance, time or priority to his/her weaknesses or areas of development. If your child is different, respect his/her uniqueness and learn how you can help to develop it.

Be firm about rules, regulations, expectations and consequences; however, always communicate and explain what they mean. Always be realistic about your expectations, keeping in mind the individuality and age of the child. Help your children to learn how to be accountable for their actions and teach them how to accept the consequences for what they do.

Always encourage children to be independent and not to blindly accept what they are taught, if they feel it is not right or they don't understand. Teach them to question. Irrespective of how many times they fail, fall or make mistakes, let them learn from errors and to cope with them. Correcting them harshly or demoralizing them when they make mistakes is very detrimental to their learning or development.

Consciously or subconsciously, stop comparing children to their siblings, peers or yourselves. They will not be able to deal with peer pressure, competition or defeat. Let them know that it is not important to be the best or win all the time or come first in everything. What is important is taking part, competing healthily, working hard, trying their best and accepting failure or defeat. What is most important is that they should feel encouraged about doing their best and to be happy for their friends who have achieved more than them.

Teach your children to reach their potential and maximize their strengths and interests. Mask your disappointment if your expectations have not been met. Be positive about every activity they undertake. Never let them feel that your love is based on fulfilling your expectations, which is the worst kind of feeling to have while growing up. Unconditional love is what they need.

Encourage excellence without being influenced by everybody else around you. Do not succumb to pressures or let the anxieties of other parents or the rigours of the educational system get to you. Every child is different, with different rates of development and unique learning curves.

Enlighten yourself as a parent—first address the fact and accept that you are not perfect and that no human being ever is! There is no perfect child, no perfect parent and no perfect 'parenting rules'. Follow your intuition and gut feelings about how to deal with situations every day. The magic is about being in tune and perfectly in sync with your child's needs, emotionally and psychologically. Everything else will then follow smoothly. Your child deserves to be happy first, and then only will his/her potential and strengths accelerate and grow. Children need to feel secure, accepted and loved 'unconditionally', but of course, that is then hoping to achieve almost perfect parenting skills!

There is almost always a hidden beauty and innocence in the imperfections our children possess. Enjoy a positive relationship with your children while they are still with you, accepting and loving them for what they are.

Chapter 2

WHY ME?

Bullying and Peer Pressure

'Nothing is so strong as gentleness,
and nothing is so gentle as real strength.'
—Ralph W. Sockman

Note found behind the maths notebook of a class eight student:

I hate school. I don't feel like even entering my classroom.
Vishal has turned the whole class against me. Just because I
told Danesh that Vishal had a crush on Alekha from the
other class section, he got pissed off. Last month, when he
found this out he abused me and threatened to bash me up.
The next day when I was in the bathroom, Vishal and four
of his close buddies caught me there and confronted me.
They asked if I had told anyone else about his crush on
Alekha. When I said no, they didn't believe me and one of
them punched me in my stomach. When I yelled back, they
pinned me against the wall and Vishal slapped me hard on
my face twice. It hurt badly, but although I felt like crying,
I controlled myself. A senior boy from class ten, whose name
I didn't know asked me to pull down my pants. He said they
wanted to make sure that I had a male organ, that I really
was a boy. They all started laughing when I said 'sorry'. I
was really scared then and thought I was going to faint.
When the school counsellor had a talk about bullying and
abuse in our school last year, I thought that it would never

happen to me. I was so happy and secure. Vishal was my best friend.

I think they felt sorry for me and let me go. However, whenever this senior boy sees me, he abuses and threatens me. When I was in the bathroom to wash up and he happened to be there, he squeezed my private parts really hard and started laughing, saying that I had a very 'small dick'. I am so ashamed and guilty. I can never tell anyone. They even told me that if I complained, they would hurt my younger sister who is in the same school bus as us. This horrible situation is my entire fault. I should have never said anything. I don't know what to do. When I enter the classroom, almost the entire class ignores me and calls me a 'loser'. The girls think I am cheap and that I have spread rumours about Alekha. When I am at home I sometimes get ten to fifteen blank calls on my landline. When I pick up the phone, the caller laughs mockingly or insults me.

Whenever I pass by, kids in my class whisper about me or laugh at me. They have spread so many rumours about me that even junior students in the bus tease me. A few days back I even tried to talk to Vishal and apologize again. He just made a face and told me to get lost. I keep thinking of how to make things better, but I don't know how to. I keep thinking of how to take revenge on these children one day. I have started hating them. I feel like screaming, yelling, shouting, but no one will hear me. No one says 'Hi' to me. No one even looks at me! They have stopped inviting me for parties and birthday celebrations. To taunt me, they purposely discuss their plans or talk of how much fun they have when they meet. I can't even study for my unit tests. I can't sleep at night and I do not feel like eating. Maybe if I pretend to be really sick, my parents won't send me to school for a few days. I even get weird thoughts of how to hurt myself or *purposely fracture my arm or leg, so that I don't have to go to school. How can I tell them that I want to change my school? I sometimes feel like killing myself. I can't believe how cruel they can be. My worst fear in life has come true. These were my best friends. We have gone for holidays together and have had so many sleepover at my house. Our parents also know each other. But I don't even have one friend. I feel so alone. I don't think I have done something that bad or wrong to receive so much hatred from them. I feel my life is over. I can't understand why this is happening to me. Why me? Why me?*

The worst thing that ever happened was last week. Vishal and his gang pretended to be nice to me for a day and said that things were cool now. They asked me to come over to another friend's house that evening. I was so excited and relieved. I felt this trial was finally over. When I went over, they started taunting and teasing me. They again asked me dirty questions. They accused me of being a troublemaker and a liar. When I tried to defend myself, Vishal got aggressive and threatened to slap me again. Someone in the room was taking a video of all of this on their cell phone, I think. Vishal then pushed me around and slapped me three, four times after I pushed him back. I started crying and vaguely remember running away from the house. I was meant to be there until dinner, but did not know what to say to my parents, so I walked along Marine Drive for three hours, until my driver came to fetch me. On that walk I must have thought of jumping into the sea almost ten times. I don't know what stopped me. I have stopped believing in God. I think I hate him too...

This class eight student eventually failed in most of his unit tests. His parents took him from one doctor to another, for various medical concerns. He complained of severe abdominal and bone pains, evening headaches and loss of appetite. He told his parents that he was bleeding from his nose. His vigilant maths teacher chanced upon his note behind his book and took it to the headmistress who informed his parents. They are now looking into what legal recourse is available. The school has taken a tough stand on grounds of sexual harassment, and has suspended the bullies.

*

Bullying often slips the parental radar because of the shame and fear that ride high in the victims. Emotional, verbal, physical or cyber bullying leave a lasting mark on most children.

In the world over, in our country and in the city, approximately 30–70 per cent of schoolgoing children have experienced bullying in some form or the other. However, only 20–40 per cent report it.

Warning signs that teachers or parents need to look out for, in children who are victims:

- Withdrawn behaviour
- Over-apologetic, irritable, showing mood swings, aggression or acting out
- Hypersensitivity, crying spells and emotional outbursts on the slightest provocation
- Low self-confidence, self-esteem, and self-worth
- Lack or loss of interest, drive or motivation in academic or co-curricular activities
- Higher levels of discord, rivalry or jealousy where siblings are concerned
- Reluctance to go to school and psychosomatic symptoms (headaches, stomach aches, cramps, not feeling unwell and so on)

- Disturbed sleeping or eating patterns, bedwetting
- Suicidal ideations or depressive symptoms

Psychology of a Bully

Why do bullies bully? It is difficult to pinpoint the clear reason why some children can be cruel, lack empathy or behave in a way that causes pain to others, sometimes just for 'fun'.

It could perhaps just be a behavioural pattern based on the narcissistic personality of certain children who always have their way or are always used to getting what they want. They force conformity and assert power so as to enhance control and manipulation in a group setting.

Some bullies are miserable themselves—often they are children from dysfunctional homes or those who may have been victims of abuse or bullying themselves. Thus they wear a mask of dominance and importance to hide or deflect their own complexes, insecurities, weaknesses or psychological turmoil.

Some bullies may have experienced social exclusion, ostracization, rejection or peer pressure in some way or the other. Being perceived as different themselves, they usually target children they see as different or weaker. Their self-esteem and self-worth go up when they put others down. They feel in control for once. Perhaps in other situations in their lives they do not have much of a say or control. Some bullies may have parents with extreme parenting styles as well, either too authoritative or over-permissive.

What Do We, as Parents, Need To Do?

From the early life of your child, instil values and the importance of being considerate where others' feelings are concerned.

Teach the child to be accepting and show tolerance to various people out there in the world devoid of discrimination, bias or hatred for any gender, religion, creed, caste, disability or skin colour.

Be effective role models as parents first, in order to set an example. Constantly create sensitivity, vigilance and awareness in schools and other educational set-ups by participating in regular workshops, talks or discussions in classrooms.

Inculcate the concept of 'collective responsibility' so that students completely understand the effects of bullying peers, the outcomes, and shortcomings or weaknesses of the 'by-standers' who either join in the fun or do nothing to stop it.

Constantly reinforce the need to stand up for what is right and always undo what is wrong, no matter how close the child may be to the person causing pain to others. That will strengthen character too.

Participate in setting up anti-ragging squads, monitoring systems or a disciplinary cell within the school itself with clear disciplinary policies and consequences in place. Schools should also be prepared to handle legal ramifications regarding serious offences, cyber bullying or sexual harassment.

Insights for Parents

Always pay close attention, be alert and listen to what your child is trying to say to you, leaving channels of communication open. Look out for warning signs and understand that your child may not come to you first and talk to you about any unpleasant situation. The child could be feeling embarrassed, inadequate and low on self-confidence; perhaps experiencing anxiety and fear too. Thus ego does not permit a child to report or complain. Reporting would mean accepting and telling others about his own weaknesses or inability to be strong and stand up for himself.

Never ask direct questions or overreact. Appear calm,

collected and in control so as to further instil security, and a sense of calm and well-being in your child.

Start with an 'identification' process, in which you talk about your own past experiences, how you got hurt or bullied or lost out on friendships or what your own weaknesses were, so that your child does not feel alone, but understood. This may help the child feel more comfortable in sharing his own experiences with you.

Let the child know that someone else's behaviour is not his fault or weakness. Explain the psychology of a bully to him. This is very important to dissipate the anger or hatred felt towards the bully. Revenge or hatred is never a solution.

To make him feel safer and more confident, tell him that you will take the matter forward and do exactly what he wants you to do. An impulsive or emotional reaction would only make the situation far worse for your child.

Always seek professional guidance through the school counsellor to get another perspective and be equipped to handle the situation better. The bully, victim, and bystanders need to be counselled or spoken with. Sometimes your child may find it more comforting to speak to someone more objective, someone other than you. Please allow or encourage counselling. Do not feel let down as a parent nor any guilt for being unable to help earlier.

Let your child know that you are proud of him and that you think that he's brave and strong. Also let him know that you love him just a little bit more today.

Chapter 3

COPING WITH A DIFFERENCE
Learning Disabilities and ADHD

> *'All children are gifted…some just open their presents later than others…'*
> —Unknown

Dear Parents,

I am the mother of a thirteen-year-old beautiful and sensitive boy. He was born full-term with no problems or complications before, during or after the delivery. He was the first baby born into our enormous joint family and I think there may have been at least twenty people waiting eagerly for his arrival at the Breach Candy hospital that night. Apart from the usual colic and reflux, he was a perfect baby who even clocked himself into a good eating and sleeping routine. He had big round eyes, was chubby with deep dimples on his cheeks and gurgled with delight when shown new toys or introduced to new food. He was playful and curious and all his developmental milestones were age-appropriate. He even spoke in full sentences by the time he was two and a half years of age. In his nursery school, I was told that he was grasping concepts well, he had good social skills and that his fine motor skills were emerging.

One consistent feedback to me from his teachers was that he was a very 'active' child. Little did I know at that time that this seemingly harmless feedback would soon be used *against him in a couple of years and that he would be labelled as 'hyperactive'.*

By the end of class one, I was told by his class teacher that he was very restless and found it difficult to sit in one place. His work was often incomplete and he lacked an age-appropriate attention span, basic concentration levels, and focus. He was sometimes in such a hurry to complete his work that he ended up making the silliest of mistakes with spellings and grammar.

His impulsiveness started worsening and getting him into fights and trouble with his peers. He would get impatient while playing games and could not wait for his turn. I was called into school on two occasions as he had pushed and scratched a few boys in his class. I kept trying to ask him what was going on with him and I kept getting different reasons—to a point where I realized he did not know why he behaved as he did.

He would often get reprimanded or get adverse remarks in his school diary. I was then asked by the school to give them permission to keep him back for 'detention' so he would feel more accountable and responsible for his work. That only made him resent studies and the school more. Towards the end of the year, the principal called my husband and me for a meeting to discuss Rohaan and his progress.

We were then advised by their team that repeating the year for him would be in his best interest as he was not at the class level of functioning and that there were many lags. We were told that it would strengthen his basic foundation skills to prepare him better for class two. We were also told that his attitude and behavioural issues did not help the situation either. I was heartbroken. My son in the traditional sense had 'failed' the year in class one! He would be kept back a year while all his peers and friends would be in a higher class. I froze, despite a hundred questions whirling in my head. How could they do this to my child? Why had they not let me know all this sooner? Why couldn't the teachers make an effective change in my child? What would other parents and children in his batch think or say? Was the school guiding me correctly or merely finding an easy way out to deal with Rohaan?

I did not sleep that night. Blame and guilt kept eating me up from within. Self-doubt went on for months and months thereafter. But what frustrated me the most was the guilt. Was I a good enough mother? Had I not taught him in the right manner? Shouldn't I have picked up or sensed these warning signs? Was it too late to undo the damage? What would my family or friends think of me? How was I to begin helping my child? Should I change his school or let him repeat the year? If I were to change schools, which one would accept him? Who would give admission to a weak student? Besides, my son was in one of Mumbai's best schools.

I believed that at such a young age, children were meant to come home after a full day of school to relax, then play, learn a sport or to play an instrument, go to a friend's house, kick a ball, bicycle around the building or sometimes just be at home building Lego, doing a puzzle, painting or chilling in front of the TV.

In desperation, I took the impulsive decision to let Rohaan repeat the year. I felt at that moment there was no choice, nor did I have a better solution. Yet instinctively I knew I was making the wrong decision and that something wasn't right. I knew deep within, intuitively, that my son was not okay but I did not want to accept that in my mind.

The following year got even worse and matters started

plummeting downhill further. My son was constantly being compared to my nephew who was a year younger to him. My husband started doing the same. He also blamed me along with other family members, insinuating that I probably wasn't doing enough academic work with Rohaan, or that maybe I was not teaching him correctly.

How could I tell them that Rohaan and I sat over fifteen minutes of homework for more than two hours and still could not complete it? How could I explain to them that he would make the same spelling error over and over again after my teaching the same word to him in perhaps ten different ways? We even etched those words with our fingers over the condensed water on the bathroom mirror, after a shower. How could I make them understand that when I took up his work orally he was brilliant, and had good command over his spoken language and vocabulary. When the same content had to be put down and transferred into writing, everything would go wrong. His sequencing and concepts would be jumbled up. Sentence structure and grammar would be wrong. Spelling errors would crop up time and again, and most questions would not be comprehended.

One issue was causing most of his problems: he could not understand what he was reading. This was leading to all the anxiety and frustration, and the reluctance to read or do any written work. My son's handwriting deteriorated and the content of his written expression was still way below his class level. How could I tell my family that there were more problems and complaints surfacing in school? Rohaan was not adjusting well to his new peers. He got into more fights in class. In the school bus, his old friends started teasing and ragging him, calling him names, abusing him and ridiculing him. 'Loser' and 'failure' were the most common words used for him. Complaints of his distracting the class, not completing his work and mocking his teachers had become an almost daily feature.

At this point, I started losing control of my emotions. I was angry and frustrated, mostly in denial. I was shouting and yelling at my son all the time. I dreaded 4 p.m.—the time when he would return home. I started hating the ritual of unzipping his heavy school bag, removing his tattered diary, reviewing and planning his daily homework, then calling a few of his classmates' mothers (which was most embarrassing) to find out what work he had missed. Some mothers would not even come on the line and would avoid taking my calls. Whom was I to turn to?

There were dark moments when I started hating my own child. I was disgusted with him. I could not understand or fathom why he was the way he was. At this point, I was fighting with my husband a lot and had spoilt my relationship with my sister-in-law who was really close to me at one time. I even started blaming my husband and his family for Rohaan's problems. I had begun turning neurotic. All the dreams that I had about my child started to shatter and fade. I was getting anxiety attacks and could not deal with his imperfections. At this point, I even started whacking and slapping him. Every time I struck him over studies, I think a little piece within me died too. I was seeing him as everybody else had perceived him, even though I was his mother. Nothing seemed to work, not even the tutor who I had employed for a couple of weeks.

Then, one evening, while helping him study for an EVS assessment, his belligerence and defiance got worse. In that impulsive moment at the dining table I reached out to the *nearest object, which happened to be a huge glass fruit bowl. Within seconds it lay in both my hands, and I indicated that I planned to smash it over Rohaan's head. He was only seven years old. I will never forget his eyes. They were filled with shock, disbelief and fear. All this while, no matter what we said or how I punished him or yelled at him, there was never any real fear. And now, his terror was palpable.*

I had vowed never to bring my child up the way I had been. Growing up for me was associated with the worst memories. My parents would hit my siblings and me really hard for just about anything—whether it was misbehaviour, not eating properly, making a noise or not getting high marks. I remember, once my brother and I were thrashed for disturbing my parents during an afternoon nap. I was becoming like them. My genes were getting the better of me.

Both Rohaan and I wept ourselves to sleep that night. He woke up a couple of times with bad dreams. That was when he started bedwetting, soiling his clothes at least twice a week, if not more. The situation was going drastically wrong and it was time to take some serious action.

I contacted my paediatrician who gave me the number of a child psychiatrist and psychotherapist. My husband refused to come for the appointment. He fought with me that morning, claiming that I needed the shrink more than my son did. So I went alone with a lot of apprehension and nervousness. What was I going to tell him, what would he ask, how much should I share...? There were yet again hundred questions swirling in my head.

Within the first two minutes of our appointment I started weeping uncontrollably and continued doing so during the entire session, while relating my story to the child psychiatrist. Since it was the beginning, it was cathartic. I cannot begin to express how light I was already feeling while he was explaining, talking, clearing doubts and giving me clarity with answers. For the first time things about Rohaan seemed to make sense. I could now perhaps understand what he was going through and what his symptoms meant. For the first time a solution was to be generated by a professional. For the first time somebody 'empathized' with my situation and what I was going through.

The psychiatrist gave me a provisional diagnosis of a learning disability (dyslexia) with ADHD (Attention Deficit Hyperactive Disorder, which is characterized by difficulty in sustaining attention and hyperactivity). I had heard about dyslexia before but didn't know much about it or about ADHD. I went home that day and spent three hours reading information from the internet. Everything I read about learning difficulties and ADHD seemed to reflect Rohaan's symptoms. I could identify with all the warning signs and behaviour patterns.

I wept again. Now I knew. I had some understanding and some answers.

The following week, Rohaan went through the entire battery of educational tests and clinical assessments to diagnose his difficulties and understand his other areas of strength, weakness and potential. It was confirmed in a few weeks later that Rohaan had dyslexia, a disability with reading and comprehension, as well as dysgraphia, a disability that hampered written expression. He also had ADHD.

I went back home with my son and all the reports. He asked me for the first time, 'Mom, what's wrong with me?' I did not break down. I now had to be strong for him. I had to walk the path and go through this journey with him. I hugged him and told him that he had a brilliant non-

conventional mind. I also told him that no one was perfect and that everybody had strengths and weaknesses. I said, 'Look at me!' And then we both laughed. We knew we needed to work on his language, spellings, reading and writing.

Later that night, I broke down into bitter tears on my husband's shoulder. We spoke for hours after. He accompanied me to the psychiatrist for many sessions then on to understand Rohaan better.

To my horror, when we met the principal of his school, she refused to empathize with Rohaan's learning difficulties. She barely glanced through the reports and then asked why we hadn't approached the school first. She said that the school had its own psychologist and that they would need her review as well. Then she actually insinuated that it was up to Rohaan to overcome his difficulties. She said that if Rohaan changed his attitude and focused better in class, he could do far better as he was extremely intelligent. She even indirectly asked us if things were all right at home!

This is when it suddenly dawned on me that the school was not the place for him anymore. This was not where he belonged. He could never be integrated into a conventional, mainstream, run-of-the mill education system. He needed something different. I do not know what came over me that day or where I mustered up the strength. I told the principal that Rohaan had not failed. The system had failed him. The school had failed him. He was not understood well enough. His different learning needs were not addressed at all. I then, without much else to say, asked for his school-leaving certificate and walked out of her office.

As for my little boy, his spirit had broken and his confidence was extremely low. He barely maintained eye contact with new people met. He stopped going out to play with his building friends. His nightmares and bedwetting continued and his behavioural problems remained the same. He had mood swings, remaining frustrated for most parts of the day and whining for the smallest of things. He took no responsibility and gained no independence. His maturity levels seemed to regress. I realized through his counsellor that his behavioural issues were perhaps defences to keep him going and displace the focus and attention away from his learning struggles.

Then Rohaan gave me hope when he asked me a couple of days later, 'Mom, can I go to a new school?'

He is now in a different school that integrates children with different learning needs. It took me over two months to make this decision for my child. This decision was made much against my larger family's wishes—only my husband and Rohaan were with me on this.

Rohaan's new school is very small in comparison to most others. There are never more than ten students in a class. This allows him to get individual attention from teachers. It also allows him to express himself and be himself. His symptoms and behaviour patterns are understood. The teachers do not berate him for his performance or for answering out of turn. He is not humiliated for asking multiple questions in class and not given detention for incomplete classwork or homework. He is not embarrassed by his peers for giving a wrong answer.

Rather, Rohaan is taught to respect others around him and understand their strengths and weaknesses too. There is no tolerance for ridicule or bullying. Classes are held to build the students' social skills and personalities. The focus is more on emotional and psychological development and well-being rather than on marks or ranks.

Rohaan's teachers, irrespective of the subjects they teach, are special educators who teach him in a way he understands. They teach him at his pace and his level of comprehension. They focus more on his strengths and capabilities rather than constantly worrying or complaining about what he cannot do. They encourage him to think beyond a textbook and offer a holistic curriculum with daily co-curricular activities and sports. All other interventions—especially occupational therapy and sensory integration therapy—are given to children during school hours itself.

These days, Rohaan and I do not sit for hours over homework—which he now does independently after just over one and a half years of attending this school. We do not fight over assessments. He does not have to rely on rote-learning. He understands what he reads now and has ample time to work on his skills, even though they are behind his chronological age and the expected norm.

Rohaan is motivated and challenged, confident and happy. He is active and curious, excited and eager. Most importantly, he is 'happy'…I have my little boy's spirit back. I have my husband, family and sanity back.

Rohaan laughs, jokes and plays more than ever. He has time. His morning stomach aches and headaches have gone. He sleeps and eats better and his bedwetting is almost gone. He's made close friends. He loves showing me all the positive reinforcements, stickers and certificates that he earns from school that encourage him to do better and better.

On his first Annual Day last week, Rohaan was called onto the stage for the first time in his life, and awarded a Certificate for 'Intellect beyond Curriculum' and a Progress Certificate in English. I cried again, but they were tears of pride and joy. I felt so small in comparison to what he had achieved at such a young age despite having so many challenges or 'disabilities'. That night while tucking him into bed, half asleep, he turned around and placed his little hand around my neck and whispered, 'I love you, Mom...'

That is all I needed. I've accepted and understood him for who he was and what he is. I've learned to accept and love him unconditionally. It has been a journey, a learning path. I look at him and know what he stands for. By not focusing on what he cannot do and all the imperfections he is riddled with, I have allowed him to grow into what he can be, instead of what he could never become...Who is perfect? Does such a person exist?

I hope that every mother, every parent, no matter how hard it is, does the same for their child...

An enlightened parent

Learning Disabilities

Learning disabilities include a variety of disorders that affect the acquisition, retention, understanding, organization or use of verbal and or non-verbal information. They may also cause difficulties with organization skills, time management, social perception, and social interaction. These are not intellectual disabilities. In fact, many individuals who have been diagnosed with learning disabilities have high to superior levels of intelligence.

Learning disabilities may cause impairments that are life-long. However with early diagnosis and intervention, consistent therapies with a multi-disciplinary approach and alternative, differentiated teaching methodologies and remediation, the outcomes, achievements and progress of these learners are overwhelming.

Also, the human brain has an amazing ability called neuro-plasticity—essentially, changes in neural and learning pathways of the brain due to changes in behaviour, environment, processing and thinking. New learning pathways and better functional organization can be initiated with the right strategies and stimuli. This may also improve cognitive functioning and memory.

Learning disabilities affect 10 per cent of the world's population, making this cohort the single largest disabled population today. Approximately 13–14 per cent of all school-going children in India, with 27 lakh people in Mumbai itself, have these difficulties. About 35 per cent of students with learning disabilities supposedly drop out of schools and almost 50 per cent of adolescent suicides have been by learning-disabled young people.

Most children with these disabilities have emotional, behavioural or psychological difficulties. Most are afflicted with stress and anxiety, poor self-esteem and confidence, low motivation and drive, poor coping mechanisms and life skills.

Due to the wide and varied manifestations of learning disabilities with comorbid diagnostics, very few children are identified early. This is also due to a paucity of experienced teachers, counsellors or professionals trained in this field, who can identify or diagnose early warning signs and symptoms. Schools today have high student–teacher ratios, with vast academic content, less time and high competitive levels, making it even more difficult for a child with different learning abilities. Therapies, remedial intervention and counselling, which are parts of the multi-disciplinary treatment process, thus take a back seat because of time constraints.

Causes of Learning Disabilities

Learning disabilities are linked to genetic factors, or congenital and or neuro-biological factors. They are not linked to cultural or language differences, socio-economic background, psychological, emotional or personality-based factors (such as lack of motivation). Let's consider some of the causes of learning disabilities:

Specific deficits in the left frontotemporal region of the brain or typical asymmetries in the left perisylvian region of the brain, which is related to language processing. A smaller left hemisphere of the brain or a larger right hemisphere may also cause these disabilities as does an under-developed cerebellum.

Poor foetal brain development or low birth weight can lead to difficulty in learning. Other causes are oxygen deprivation at birth, pre-term delivery, seizures, haemorrhages, alcohol or drug abuse by the child's mother during pregnancy, Vitamin B_1 and choline deficiency, lead poisoning.

Other causes are medications for allergies, asthma, rhinitis, steroids and chemotherapy; congenital problems; genetic and hereditary factors; head injuries, accidents and malnutrition.

Warning Signs of Learning Disabilities

Here are some signs you should look out for, if you're concerned that your child might have learning difficulties:

- Is intelligent and is sometimes also gifted
- Tight, awkward pencil grip, and body position
- Illegible handwriting
- Omitted words in sentences
- Difficulty in organizing thoughts
- Difficulty with grammar
- Short attention span
- Poor listening skills
- Trouble with following instructions
- Confuses left and right
- Poor motor coordination

- Immature behaviour
- Produces reversals and rotations of alphabets
- General disorganization
- Inconsistent behaviour and work
- Displays exceptional ability in sports, arts, science, and verbalization

Types of Learning Disabilities

Dyslexia

This learning disability is characterized by difficulty in processing language (particularly in school-going children) and problems with phonological processing, spelling, naming, speed, and working memory.

It often manifests itself in the child, showing difficulty in visual processing or in auditory processing.

The child has normal intelligence, articulation and communication, but is slow in reading, often interchanging letters within a word, confusing letters such as b, d, p, q and sound-letter associations. He/she has good oral and verbal expression, but faces problems with written expression. It is because of reading and writing problems, particularly finding it difficult to recognize words and understanding their meanings. A dyslexic child performs poorly in academic activities, with fluctuations and discrepancies. Poor vocabulary, slow automatic naming and errors in spelling are signs of this condition as are poor analytical and abstract thinking skills, memory and recall, planning, organizing, and structuring.

Proficiency and speed of comprehension are affected, so information processing is problematic. Auditory, visual or kinaesthetic learning may be affected too.

Dysgraphia

In dysgraphia, the child has difficulty in written expression. There are three types of dysgraphia:

Dyslexic dysgraphia in which spontaneous writing is illegible, although drawing and copying are normal; motor dysgraphia or the condition where motor problems cause illegible automatic or copied written expression; and spatial dysgraphia, which is characterized by poor understanding of the concept of space.

Dyspraxia

Typical problems in this condition are related to fine motor skills (10 per cent of the population). There are problems with eye–hand coordination, control of movement, planning or execution of complex movements. Other signs are lack of directional and spatial awareness, poor balance, poor fine and gross motor coordination, posture and tactile discomfort. The child often has difficulty in speech, resulting in impatience and frustration.

Dyscalculia

This condition means that the child faces difficulty in working out arithmetic operations and related concepts. There is dysfunction in the reception and comprehension of specific mathematical tasks. As a result, problems with concepts of time, direction, and money affect the child as do poor long-term memory, and poor ability to visualize maps and diagrams.

In a type of dyscalculia called pseudo-dyscalculia, emotional block and anxiety regarding mathematics manifest. In acalculia (brain damage) or post-lesion dyscalculia, disability in mathematics is caused by a head injury, brain tumour or other physical trauma.

Attention Deficit Hyperactive Disorder (ADHD)

Every child who is hyperactive or has problems focusing and sustaining the attention span is not an ADHD child. This is one of the most over-diagnosed conditions in children. Treatments, therapies or medications thus need to be implemented only after thorough evaluation of whether the child's academic or social functioning is drastically affected. One should intervene when a child's true intellectual and academic potential is not achieved owing to this condition.

The *DSM IV* (*Diagnostic and Statistical Manual of Mental Disorders*) contains the diagnostic criteria for the most common mental disorders. The criteria for diagnosing ADHD is broadly divided into three categories:

1. Inattention: The child often fails to pay close attention to details or makes careless mistakes in class and other work. The problems include sustaining attention in play activities and a reluctance to engage in tasks that require focused attention like classwork or homework. The child is easily distracted by extraneous stimuli and is often forgetful in daily activities. He/she does not seem to listen when spoken to directly, often loses things (toys, books, pencils, assignments among other items) and finds it difficult to organize tasks and activities.

2. Hyperactivity: A hyperactive child fidgets with hands or feet or squirms when seated, and does not remain in one place even when other children sit still as expected or required, such as when a class is being held. Restlessness, an inability to play or engage in leisure activities quietly, talking excessively and always being 'on the go' are other signs.

3. Impulsiveness: The child finds it difficult to wait for his/

her turn in games or group situations and often interrupts others or intrudes on others' activities. He/she also blurts out answers to questions before they have been completed.

What You Need to Do as a Parent

Early diagnosis, evaluation and intervention are the keys to better prognosis. Brain plasticity/neuroplasticity refers to the brain's natural lifelong ability to change, form new connections and generate new brain cells in response to experience and learning to re-train the brain so, parents should ensure the correct therapy is used for the child.

A complete and comprehensive evaluation of the child, using psycho-educational methods and employing standardized tests is essential. This gives clear indication of the child's potential, strengths and weaknesses. These tests are age-specific and give clarity to the lags in specific academic areas, thus giving a clear diagnosis of the specific learning disability. A multi-disciplinary team approach should be followed. The team should include a developmental paediatrician, child psychiatrist, clinical psychologist, special educator, occupational therapist, speech and language therapist and physiotherapist.

Audiometric and ophthalmological examinations should be carried out. Medical examinations are essential to rule out underlying health issues. Psychological, social and behavioural evaluations for the child are also needed.

Parental counselling and case discussions need to follow the evaluation so that a clear path of interventions or therapies can be visualized. Awareness, recognition, research, and self-education by parents is most effective. This can be done through counselling, attending workshops or lectures, internet research or parent support groups.

Approach school authorities for available exemptions or

concessions. Schools should be sensitized to each child's learning needs. Teach the child organizational skills, study skills, different learning strategies, making and following a timetable and management skills. Constantly foster positive feelings of self-esteem, confidence and hope in your child without comparing his/her performance with any other child.

Do not get frustrated, but persevere with your efforts to help your child. Trusting, reposing faith in and being patient with people who are helping you are of great importance. Do not end up hopping from one therapist or doctor to another. These processes take time and require patience. Try to bestow your faith, trust and belief in the team you have chosen for your child. Achievements and improvements take a long while and each child reaches milestones in different ways and in his/her own time.

Battling the Anxiety Associated with Learning Disabilities

Every parent has a dream-child concept. It is a narcissistic, almost selfish and obsessive thought process that each of us has. We dream that our progeny will possess the best of our genes to be perfect in looks, features, intellect, personality, behaviour, relationships, health, achievements and other attributes important to their lives.

Parents often wish that every dream they could not fulfil or complete in their lifetimes, will be accomplished by their children. We, as parents, want them to be the best in everything. This brings about unrealistic expectations and non-acceptance when a problem with the child does arise.

There is fear and denial if a child's development is not in accordance with accepted milestones. There is always an inner voice, a gut feeling and intuition that something is not right. Non-acceptance thus starts becoming an internal defence to protect parents from the impact of reality. A hope that it will just go away, get better or change is also part of this reaction.

Social factors, stigmas and family pressures with the fear of being blamed for it, make it even more difficult to accept a child's disability.

Most parents go through a phase of denial, disbelief, doubt, and blame. This then progresses to shame, guilt, self-pity, grief and losing hope, which lead to frustration, anger, rage, panic, and anxiety. Embarrassment about the child's behaviour and resentment of the child are also common.

Listen to your own inner voice and beliefs. Trust a professional to guide you with realistic goals and expectations. Do not battle with yourself, your spouse, family members, teachers or the school.

Do not embark upon a blame game or make it your life's mission to find the reason, cause or the treatment for the disability. There is no quick fix and sometimes no answers to inner questions. This will only lead to more frustration and isolation.

Take opportunities for breaks, both for you and your child. Your emotional balance, patience, peace of mind, and coping mechanisms as a parent are the keys to your child's progress and achievements. Do not neglect other duties, routines and especially your other children. Do not neglect yourself either. Do not compromise on free time, play, extracurricular activities, music or sport. These aspects are equally important for you and your child.

Be prepared for uneducated questions asked by family members or friends. Be prepared for your child's questions regarding his/her disability as well. Answer them age-appropriately, intelligently, tactfully and positively, always giving hope, encouragement and confidence. Let your child know that you are a team and will fight the disability together. Always let your child know that no one is perfect. Everyone has strengths and weaknesses. Even you!

Never compare his/her progress or performance with other children, siblings or children with different learning abilities who study in the same class. Never treat him/her differently or like a special child. Bring about complete normality within all environments. This will instil further confidence, independence, and a sense of responsibility.

You will have to let go of your child one day. And when that day comes you will want him/her to have independence and courage. Every problem is solvable and every challenge or obstacle in life can be overcome. Ensure that your child has healthy coping mechanisms, independence, and the ability to live life with the most important and constant gift that you leave him/her, which is true inner happiness and peace of mind.

Chapter 4

CAREGIVER'S ANXIETY

Borderline Personality Disorder

'Often, it's not about becoming a new person,
but becoming the person you were meant to be, and already are,
but don't know how to be...'
—Heath L. Buckmaster

Case Study

25 August 2012, Saturday 5 p.m.

One day, Mr and Mrs Kaul came to my clinic to consult me about their twenty-one-year old son Ari. They appeared distraught and his mother could barely speak as she was choking with emotions she could not contain. The father did most of the speaking, trying to be as calm as possible, but with a dead, helpless look in his eyes and a tremor in his voice. They had taken an appointment because the situation in their home was beyond their control. For over a year Ari's behaviour was getting more and more difficult to manage. His anger and bouts of rage were increasing in frequency and intensity. They described him as always restless and on the edge. His father said that anything could trigger him off. He had broken a few things in the house, recently smashed his computer and tore his clothes on three occasions because the housemaid had not ironed them as he had wanted.

They looked ashamed and embarrassed while relating one incident after another. If he did not like the food cooked at home, he would get into an argument with his mother, using abusive words. If his father intervened, he would hurl dishes across the dining room, smashing plates and scattering food all over the walls and floor. Two weeks earlier, Ari got into the family car, but on the way realized that the petrol tank was nearly empty. He called his father over the mobile phone and started abusing him. When his father asked him to be more responsible and fill up the tank himself, he rammed the car against a wall and threw the mobile phone out of the window.

The Kauls were feeling more concerned as they claimed that he had always been a difficult child, stubborn and defiant, but was now becoming very irrational. Anything or everything irritated him. He had become extremely selfish, wanting everything to go his way. His mood swings had become extremely intense and rapid, his sleeping patterns erratic.

After the father did most of the talking, Mrs Kaul said that Ari was speaking louder and faster, becoming suspicious of people, fighting a lot with his girlfriend, not studying or submitting assignments on time and hardly attending college. Tears rolled down her cheeks as she described how one night after a fight, he went around the house picking up one beautiful glass artefact after another and smashing it on the floor in front of her in a methodical, purposeful manner. After five such expensive pieces were broken, he left the others intact, saying that he was done breaking her favourites. Some of these were antiques possessed by the family for generations.

After much reluctance, she turned to her husband and asked him to show me something. With shaking hands, he unbuttoned the top four buttons of his shirt to show me the left side of his chest and his back. It had marks, bruises and a swelling. After a close examination, I realized that a rib was fractured. In one of his rages over pocket money, Ari had tried to snatch his father's wallet, which had led to a scuffle. Then Ari completely lost control and started punching him, one blow after another. When his mother tried to stop him, he slapped her. She told me that after the incident, she had headaches and a ringing or whistle-like sound in her right ear. On examination, I discovered that her eardrum had been ruptured.

At this point Mr Kaul broke down as well. They both wept silently and uncontrollably for at least fifteen minutes, broken-hearted.

When I asked about Ari's background, they said he had completed his schooling and junior college from Mumbai and was currently pursuing an engineering degree. He was a brilliant student and top-ranker. They described him as very humorous, witty, street-smart and large-hearted. They claimed that his violent behaviour began when he was eighteen years of age. There was a two-year phase thereafter when he started going out for late night parties and coming home inebriated almost every week. His parents knew he was abusing drugs, primarily marijuana, but thought he was just experimenting with his peers.

I asked them to follow up two days later. They said they were now petrified of their own child. Mr Kaul folded both his hands before leaving, begging for a solution, saying they wanted their son back.

27 August 2012, Monday 4 p.m.

Mr and Mrs Kaul came in to discuss further investigations, intervention and treatment options. I explained that in order to make a comprehensive diagnosis, it was imperative for me to meet Ari. They needed to get a urine test done to rule out the abuse of drugs. I gave them a provisional diagnosis of a 'substance- induced disorder' that could mimic a mental illness. Alcohol, cocaine, amphetamine, hallucinogens, marijuana or opioids could have this effect. Symptoms could range from psychotic behaviour, paranoia, disorders like bipolar disorder or anxiety.

I explained that these symptoms were caused by a neuro-chemical imbalance in the brain. If it was substance-related, the symptoms would abate in a few weeks or months if the patient stopped taking drugs. I told them how the medications would work and the importance of using them on a long-term basis. They were relieved and hopeful, less anxious as their doubts were cleared. They spoke at length about Ari's childhood and claimed that the three of them had had a fairly stable family life with barely any discord, trauma or school-related problems. There was no history of any mental illness or substance-abuse in the family.

We decided to schedule an appointment with Ari and convince him to do a urine test.

30 October 2012, Tuesday, 6 p.m.

In the first session with Ari Kaul, I noticed he was charming, good-looking, witty and intelligent. It appeared that he had recently gained weight. He was rather over-friendly, smiled a lot and established a rapport quickly. However, his eye contact was fleeting and he had difficulty maintaining his attention span, concentration and focus. He spoke very rapidly with a high pitch and tone of voice. Most of his conversations were manic and about himself. It was evident that his thought process was fragmented as he jumped rapidly from one topic to another.

He was evasive whenever I touched on the topic of his parents. He kept shaking his right foot rapidly and asked if he could have a smoke. Eventually, when asked about substance abuse, he claimed he only smoked pot on weekends. He had been doing so for two years. Only if his parents provoked him or 'fucked up' his mood would he smoke up mid-week. On further probing about how his parents provoked him, he came up with a hundred inconsequential reasons, most of them irrational and extremely selfish.

He had no insight into his anger problems or his abusive behaviour. Instead, he repeatedly asked to be treated for what was his 'depression, obsessive compulsive disorder and ADHD'.

Taking a cue from that I convinced him to get a full health check-up with investigations. He then agreed to do a complete urine and blood profile. He also agreed to use ADHD medications if required, and follow up treatment regularly.

16 January 2013, Friday, 8 p.m.

Follow up with Ari Kaul. He had not followed up after his first session. His parents claimed that after the first session, he had become violent that very same night as he had felt betrayed. He claimed that his parents were evil and wanted to label him with a psychiatric disorder to tell the world that he was insane. He threatened to kill them or himself.

The second day he brought marijuana joints into the house and smoked up, as his parents sat across him.

On this follow up, he came in a dishevelled state. He sobbed and howled aloud during the session almost like a child. He said that his had been the worst childhood ever and he used to be hated and bullied in school. He also claimed that in junior college he had been sexually abused by an older student in the bathroom on campus. He said this had happened a couple of times, which had messed his mind up completely. He spoke about how his father was always controlling and dominating and never allowed him to think for himself. He said that he had to beg and plead for everything, whether it was the car, pocket money or good food. He also shared that his parents made his anger worse. Instead of backing off they would further provoke him and use foul language, which would then make him violent. He said he could not control his temper as he had the impulsive-hyperactive type of ADHD which he had mentioned in the last session. He begged to get treated, saying that he could not study or concentrate. He wanted to complete his engineering degree.

He sobbed as he told me he had just broken up with his girlfriend. He had been in nine relationships before this. He blamed her for his substance abuse and for lowering his confidence and esteem. He also spoke about how he could not get intimate with her because of his sexual abuse experience and thought he suffered from erectile dysfunction because of it.

After I made some suggestions, he agreed to stop abusing drugs and start ADHD medication. The line of treatment prescribed seemed to agree with Ari.

10 July 2013, Wednesday, 3 p.m.

Mr and Mrs Kaul came for a follow-up session. Ari was more focused on studying and now attended college. His medications, masked in his food or water, helped to control his anger, violence and emerging psychotic symptoms. These were administered by his mother and it was making a difference. The intensity and frequency of violent episodes had reduced. He had become more rational. His hyperactivity, irritability and manic symptoms had lessened. He had stopped using marijuana and was sleeping better. His mood and thought processes were more streamlined. He had become less suspicious about the world and seemed more at ease. His parents were very pleased with his progress. Told that a neuro-chemical imbalance had caused his erratic behaviour, they understood that medication had to be continued for at least two years.

11 November 2013, Thursday, 2 p.m.

Had an emergency session with Mr and Mrs Kaul today, the reason being that Ari had taken a blunt blade from his father's razor and, on the previous night, tried to slice his wrist four to five times. He did so because another girlfriend had rejected him. He told his parents he wanted to die and if he did, then she would never be able to forgive herself for dumping him. The parents claimed the gashes were superficial, but he kept insisting on being rushed to the hospital. When they refused and tried to calm him down, he again became verbally abusive and aggressive. He locked himself in the bathroom, threatening to swallow all the tablets in the cabinet and to take revenge on his parents for their insensitivity. After two hours of pleading, he came out and went off to sleep. His parents were confused about this behaviour, wondering if he was using drugs again.

18 November 2013, Thursday, 4 p.m.

Follow up with Ari. He sat down calmly and seemed preoccupied. He said he had come in because his parents had insisted. He felt they needed more help than he did. Insight-oriented therapy with rational emotive behaviour therapy did not seem to help him much. His attitude was still ego-centric and self-centred. I observed his inability to empathize; his impulsiveness, restlessness and anxiousness still persisted. He wanted to give up his ADHD medications. He also said he had decided to drop out of engineering college, which his parents had forced him to join. He had no real friends left and could not trust anyone. He had put on more weight and had started smoking cigarettes on a regular basis. He claimed that his mood was often dysphoric now, marked by anxiety and unease, and that nothing really interested him or made him happy any more—his life had become empty and meaningless. He once again brought up the intimacy issue but this time admitted he was unsure whether he was sexually abused or not as he had been on marijuana at the time and his mind was completely in a fog. He refused to talk about trying to slash his wrists, but kept repeating he was suicidal. When I suggested hospitalization, he got very uncomfortable and then angry. He thought we were all keen to put him into a mental asylum. He impulsively got up, hurled a myriad of abuses and walked out of the session, shouting that he would never come back.

15 February 2014, Friday, 7 p.m.

Joint session with the Kaul family. After much analysis and thought, I had ruled out a substance-induced psychiatric disorder, bipolar disorder or psychosis. In a very gentle manner I introduced and explained the term 'borderline personality disorder'. I told the parents that it was a pervasive pattern of instability vis-à-vis interpersonal relationships and self-image, and came with a marked display of impulsivity. Ari's history was composed of real or imagined dramatic issues, unstable multiple relationships, self-injurious behaviour or recurrent suicidal gestures or threats. He had intense episodes of irrational or illogical anger, irritability, aggression and anxiety. Stress-related paranoid ideations were also present. Later, the instability in his goals, aspirations and career plans impaired his functionality. His hostility towards his parents continued to become worse.

Ari became virtually hysterical during this joint session. He felt hurt and exposed. The reality and truth were too much to imbibe and take in. Also, his lack of empathy, social judgement and insight made it difficult for him to accept the diagnosis. He became verbally abusive yet again, hurling profanities at his parents, and walked out of the session shortly after.

His parents were broken yet again. They seemed to have lost the hope that they had gained before. They slowly realized that no substance or drug, psychosis, bipolar disorder or ADHD were to blame for his behaviour. In fact, substance abuse was common in adolescence or young adults with this disorder. No medication was going to take the symptoms of this disorder away. They felt they had nothing to hold on to.

18 June 2015, Monday, 3 p.m.

Follow up with the Kauls.

I shared with them some vital insights that have been recorded below.

How to Deal with Borderline Personality Disorders

As parents, you need to remember that in such cases, the progress, changes and improvements made will be slow and some goals difficult to achieve and fraught with apprehensions and fears. Keeping and maintaining balance is very important for your child, without expressing much appreciation during progress or negativity during relapses. The goal is to keep him/her as constructively occupied and independent as possible.

Being supportive, calm and cool is the key, always letting the child know that irrespective of his behaviour you will always be there for him. This is important as such children fear abandonment the most. However, there should be no tolerance for aggression, violence, substance abuse or self-destructive behaviour. Seek professional help when this occurs, perhaps even a rehabilitation facility.

Fears, anxieties and situations that are contrary to what they want, can drive those with borderline personality disorder to use old, unhealthy coping mechanisms. Thus relapses could include missing out on work days or school, self-mutilation or deliberate self-harm, suicidal attempts, purging or excessive drinking, substance abuse or irrational, impulsive behaviour. A parent needs to be extremely calm during these disturbing acts as they are cries for help, a way of letting others know they are in distress. Protective steps to seek professional help at that time or hospitalization are compulsory. On improvement, parents need to caution their children to move ahead slowly and take small steps towards regaining daily normal routines and schedules.

Set realistic goals after understanding and acceptance of this disorder, and take one step at a time. This will prevent extreme frustration, emotional hurt and anxiety. Focus on all the strengths that your child may have. Hidden under these are extremely deep-rooted levels of insecurity, complexes, and irrational thoughts. Thus slowly introducing potential and positive goals can prevent frustration and impatience in children as well as help re-build self-confidence. This leads to greater chances of success without frequent relapses.

Children and adolescents with borderline personality disorder have no insight into their problems and do not accept their faults. They have unhealthy or aggressive coping mechanisms, an overwhelming fear of being alone, impulse dyscontrol, fluctuating mood swings, and insecurities. It is advisable to avoid confronting them during phases of angry or violent behaviour nor get defensive or angry. This will only worsen the situation. Let the child's counsellor or psychiatrist interact with him/her during these phases. In a crisis, home visits are very useful in dissipating the worst symptoms. Consistent and regular psychotherapy, cognitive behaviour therapy and insight-oriented therapy are mandatory. This will, in time help the child realize that he/she is not always a victim or always persecuted. This will aid him/her to learn healthier coping mechanisms and control irrational and impulsive thoughts, behaviour and reactions. Therapy also helps the child manage relationships better and build on self-esteem and self-confidence. In time, this will also train him/her to think rationally and clearly, with empathy and without only ego-centric thoughts or reactions.

Maintain and sustain all family routines and bonds. Go out, take breaks, and meet friends. Talking helps a great deal. Counselling for parents is of primal importance especially since the borderline personality disorder fluctuates and varies in its symptoms tremendously. Avoid feeling isolated or victimized as parents. A parent needs to accept this disorder as one would accept any other illness in a child, no matter how hard it is. Being emotionally and psychologically strong as parents goes a long way in healing and progress. Support groups or group therapy help parents feel that they are not alone. Many ideas and valuable information can be shared, resulting in constructive strategies of dealing and coping with certain behaviour or emergencies.

Encourage your child to express feelings and emotions at the right time and place. Listening to him/her and sympathizing is the best strategy to help calm a situation. It is essential to say you believe in and love him/her no matter how hurt you have been. Be continuous and consistent with all your responses and re-enforcements. The family needs to keep a united front and be as free of conflict as possible. Make sure you give time and importance to your other children. Counselling of siblings will help them understand what this disorder means and how they need to play a key role in their sibling's progress.

Medication can help to curb risky, impulsive behaviour, self-harm or aggression. This factor must be seriously thought about and introduced as part of the treatment plan, especially during emergencies.

Chapter 5

DEAR DIARY

Teenage Crises, Eating Disorders, Experimentation and Self-harm

'Do not go where the path may lead, go instead where there is no path, and leave a trail...'
—Ralph Waldo Emerson

6 June 2011
Dear Diary,
I have just come into class ten of school and I'm freaking out. There is crazy pressure on me to perform and get high marks. My classmates feel that I could top the school and my parents have drilled it into me that I need to score 90 per cent and above! My tuition teachers keep saying that I should not let them down and this is driving me nuts.

I hate to study now. I feel like telling everybody to just back off. I don't like being compared to other kids or my cousins, but my mom and teacher keep doing it. Then they say that they're not comparing, they are just trying to motivate me by showing me examples of other children and their achievements. They say I should learn from them and study for many hours, just like they do.

I hate being called a nerd in my class. I also wish I could start wearing contact lenses. Cannot stand my thick glasses, they make me look so ugly. Aisha in class called me 'ugh' today. Guess she meant ugly. So upsetting, as I really wanted to be her friend and in their group. They call themselves 'cool' and 'the gang'. Would love to go out with them. They all have boyfriends from other schools and go out to parties. Aisha has had four boyfriends already. She said she has also 'done it' with her last boyfriend. I am sure she has as she looks real hot and thin.

I am so nervous about this year. Hope I can make more friends too. Miss my best friend. Wish she didn't have to leave our school and go to London. Feels so lonely without her. Anyway, have to study again…

28 June 2011

Just can't study or focus any more. Feel totally bored and tired all the time. I am so fed up that I could cry. No one really talks to me in class any more unless it is study-related or if they need to borrow my notes. What should I do?

I am so tired of watching TV shows or playing games on my iPad. Aisha is still being a bitch and now the other girls have joined in. They have started calling me 'the strange one'! Really don't give a shit but it hurts sometimes. Anyway, signing off to log into Facebook.

8 July 2011

I met someone on Facebook. He is from college, he said, and we chat every day. He is super cute-looking and we speak or message daily. My life has changed. He asks me many questions about myself and seems interested in my life. He is so helpful and advises me maturely on how to deal with the cool gang! He told me to hear this song called 'Cherish' and asked me to find out who sang it. Guess what? It's by a group called 'Kool & the Gang'! It is such a beautiful song. Heard it twenty times over last night… 'Let's take a walk together near the ocean shore, hand in hand you and I…let's cherish every moment we have been given, the time is passing by…'

1 August 2011

Shayan asked me to date him. I am so excited—and in love, I think. I just can't believe all this is happening so fast. I can't stop thinking of him. But I am very nervous. My mom and dad will kill me if they find out, especially since its my final year. I have stored his number on my cell phone as Shayana so they think it's a girl!

How will I meet Shayan and where? He said he does not mind coming home when my parents are not there or we could meet in my building compound. I really hope they don't find out. I told my friend Natasha about him in class today. I think she told Aisha too by the end of the day. That song keeps playing in my head. He is so romantic. His messages are so loving and caring.

I wonder how it will feel to meet him for the first time. He is damn good-looking and he excites me. I wish Aisha could see us together. She would get shocked and die of jealousy as he is sooo cute. I wonder if he would want to kiss me or not. I am so happy.

Oh, by the way, I failed in my geography test for the first time ever. My teacher was shocked and so were my friends. Haven't told my parents, they would just kill me.

30 August 2011

Met him for the third time now. He comes on his bike all the way from the suburbs to meet me. Today we went on my building terrace. I told my parents that I was going down to meet Natasha as she had to drop some notes off. He gave me this idea. He said that he loved me for the hundredth time and asked if he could kiss me. He said that the best and most private place to 'make out' was on a terrace. He said that he and his previous girlfriend used to do it on her terrace all the time. She was such a bitch, she dumped him and started dating his really close friend. Shayan said that she broke his heart, but after meeting me he does not think about her at all. He smelt really good, cologne mixed with the smell of smoke. He asked if I had ever kissed anyone before. He was gentle, but he put his tongue inside my mouth. I am not sure whether I liked that part much or not. I was confused and I felt really scared and guilty. But all my friends have apparently done it, so I was not that worried then. He touched me all over too and asked me to touch him down there but I did not. I thought we were going too fast. So he made me touch him. He held my hand down there very hard. It almost hurt me. So then I got worried and wanted to leave. I love him very much and can't think of anyone else or anything else.

'Cherish the love we have, we should cherish the life we live, cherish the love we have for as long as we both shall live, cherish the love, cherish the life...' That's our song now.

14 September 2011

My parents feel something is going on. I think they suspect me but I am being very careful. They are extremely angry and upset with my marks. They have threatened to come to school, take away my mobile or ground me. They think that Natasha and my other new friends have a bad influence on me. My parents and I have fights every day and they treat me like a child. Always nagging and suspicious, never giving me any privacy. Mum asks me such dumb questions that I get enraged. I want to be left alone.

We have been meeting the cool gang often. Aisha has become my friend and they all know about Shayan. We meet in Natasha's house for tuitions or to study and I get to speak to him from there. Aisha told us that her parents were going through a divorce and that she was messed up. That's why she was behaving like a bitch to most people. I have forgiven her now and I am so happy just to be their friend. They totally support and protect me. They help me cover up and sometimes lie to my parents as well. Shayan said he could never meet my friends as they were much younger than him and that we should keep it a secret until I was in college. My friends think I am damn gutsy and cool, and have started looking up to me.

Aisha carried some vodka to Natasha's house and we all drank it with Coke. It was super fun and we couldn't stop laughing for about an hour after. Toothpaste, mints and eye drops did the trick to hide the alcohol effect before I reached home.

26 September 2011
We fight almost daily. He feels I am immature and that I behave like a kid all the time. He also insults me if I don't call him every hour or message him. Aisha thinks that his possessiveness is too cute. He feels that our dating is meaningless unless we 'do it'. He said that all his friends make fun of him because we haven't. He sometimes yells and screams at me and asks me if there is something wrong with him. I feel sorry for him and hate myself for making him feel so bad.

My friends still haven't met him. We only meet on our terrace. He gets very rough sometimes…He has made me try his smokes and I now know how to inhale properly. I used to choke or cough at first like crazy. I have got used to it now. He said smokes will make me lose weight and that I will look sexy. He thinks I am very overweight. He said my stomach should be smaller so that my boobs look bigger. I allow him to kiss me there too. He hates my glasses too. So when we're together he always makes me remove them and I can barely see as I have a very high number. Wish I could get lenses. Hate my parents for not allowing me this.

My school principal called me to his office yesterday and asked me if everything was okay. He asked if I wanted to see the school counsellor. That's such a joke. Even Aisha and Natasha's parents were called. I don't understand why they feel that marks and studies are everything in life. Why can't they just leave us alone!

20 October 2011

I am feeling so good. I have lost seven kilos in such a short time. Our gang has been doing some reading on how to become bulimic and anorexic and lose more weight in a month. I swallow six to eight of Dad's laxative pills and throw up after my meals, especially dinner. Shayan thinks I am looking better. He slapped me today for the second time because I did not want to 'do it'. After all I have done for him and sacrificed for him, he keeps hurting me like this. I am feeling very dirty and used, and cheap. He talks only about this and I wonder whether he loves me or the sexual stuff.

I am so hurt and messed up that I feel like cutting myself as Aisha does. She has more than forty scars and cuts on her groin, below the underwear line where no one can see. She says it's the best way to cope with the emotional pain and that it makes her forget. It makes her numb and there is a pleasure in the release. Really feel like trying this with a blade.

I feel I am going crazy. I also feel like I need vodka every day to make me feel normal or happy.

I hate my parents even though I know they have done nothing wrong. Shayan blames my parents for my faults. He said that I am brainless because I allow them to control me.

He uses very filthy language when he talks to me. He called me a fucking cunt after he slapped me. I hate myself. I hate the way I look. I hate the way I feel. I love him so much, why can't he just see that? I don't know what I will do if he leaves me. I cannot live without him, I want to marry him and spend the rest of my life with him.

'I often pray before I lay down, by your side, if I receive your calling before I awake, could I make it through the night, cherish the love we have, cherish the life we live...'

1 November 2011

I have failed most of my academic tests. My parents feel they don't know who I am or what I have become. I cannot listen to their shit any more. I sometimes just feel like running away. They just don't get me. No one understands me.

Aisha's parents have divorced and her mum is relocating to Australia. I will lose my best friend again. I am so depressed. Vodka or cutting doesn't help any more. My parents dragged me to a shrink last week who diagnosed me with bulimia and started me on some meds which I spat out. I did not speak to him as I could not connect and he stared at me weirdly. I am not retarded like they think.

I cannot focus or think any more in class. My mind seems foggy and I cannot remember things. Go blank sometimes and I can't stop thinking of him. I finally Facetimed him on my iPhone without my top. He wanted to see me...he said 'I love you' after a very long time. Kind of made me feel good.

15 December 2011

I can't stop shaking...Mom and Dad are out for the weekend. Mum is receiving a Lifetime Award for her work in Delhi. There is blood everywhere. Don't know how to make it stop. Can't tell anyone, as I am so embarrassed. I think I passed

*out on the terrace but I cannot remember. Why did he leave
me? Why like that?*

*Oh God, what have I done? I am too ashamed to carry
on like this…how can I live like this…what do I tell them,
how can I explain, how will they believe or trust me ever
again…oh God, what have I done…I am so very sorry.
Please forgive me. I love you, Shayan…I always have…Mom,
Dad, none of this is your fault. I have let all of you down…*

    Love always,
    Sherry

                              *

Sherry was sixteen years old. She was hospitalized for attempted
suicide. She had lost over thirteen kilos of her body weight. Her
blood samples showed imbalances in her blood sugar levels,
haemoglobin, liver, kidney, and cardiac functions. Her vitamin
B_{12} and D_3 levels were deficient. She had high levels of marijuana-
cannabis in her urine samples. Multiple gashes cut by a blade in
her groin region were clearly visible and her menstrual periods
had not appeared for over two months. Her jaw was dislocated
from hard, multiple blows or slaps. She had been raped. Semen
samples were collected from her torn vagina. Shayan was nowhere
to be traced or found. His phone number no more existed. The
cyber crime police are still working on the case.

Sherry could not go back to school and complete class ten.
She was a straight Honours student in her school over the last
four years, but now she may have to consider home schooling.
She has many wounds that need healing. She visits her psychiatrist
every week and is on multiple medications to get back her
mental balance. She now has been allowed to wear contact
lenses. She's still very beautiful, intelligent and sensitive—and
mature. She still writes in her diary…

'The world is always changing, nothing stays the same, but love will stand the test of time. The next life that we live in, remains to be seen, will you be by my side…'

'Cherish the love we have, we should cherish the life we live, cherish the love we have, for as long as we both shall live…'

Those Anxious Teens

Data from all over the world indicate that 20–25 per cent of children and adolescents suffer from a disabling psychological, emotional or psychiatric disorder.

Suicide is the third leading cause of death amongst adolescents. The highest incidents of depression, anxiety, substance abuse, eating disorders, sexual harassment, and rape are amongst teenagers.

Why are teenagers so difficult to understand, reach out to or deal with? They lie, they shut you out, they have an attitude of superciliousness, and sometimes exude arrogance like they know it all. They are selfish and egocentric. They do not open up, find it difficult to be honest, are impulsive, and risk-takers. They are riddled with complexes and go through awkward stages, physiologically and hormonally. They are extremely insecure, moody, confused, and frustrated. They thus take relationship issues or break-ups as badly as divorcing couples or adults.

They lack self-esteem and self-confidence. The majority of adolescents hate their bodies or the way they look. They have some problem or the other; or a negative perception with their physical attributes. Teenagers are more hypersensitive than children or adults. They find it very hard to forgive or forget.

Teenagers take divorce or marital discord between their parents much more badly than younger children. On an average, teens cry at least once a week.

The Psychology of an Adolescent

Conformity

During adolescence, being one's own person normally means conforming with peers and the rules set by peer groups. Teenagers have an obsessive need to change in order to fit in, be accepted and appreciated. They will go to any lengths to feel part of the group, relenting sometimes to peer pressure without much thought or self-control. They sometimes even develop false perceptions of what is 'cool' and safe. Many adolescents begin distancing themselves from other friends and or parental control and start becoming extremely dependent on this newly-acquired group. They become defensive, protective, and possessive in relation to their new friends. They initiate talking, gestures, behaviour, dressing, attitudes, and even thinking like their peers, following role models for almost every aspect of their lives.

Identity

Around adolescence, identity is built around not just the teenagers' conception and expression of themselves, but the way they are perceived by other individuals and groups.

Teenagers go through a phase of assertion by questioning themselves, their parents or beliefs. This helps them frame their self-confidence, self-esteem, and self-worth.

Teenagers display introspective thinking—who am I? Who will I become? What are my fears? Where do I belong? These, and other such deep thoughts, shake them. Such questions cause confusion and indecision; conflict and inconsistency.

Teenagers love you (by 'you', I mean parents and other adults) and hate you. They admire and respect you and find fault(s) in you. They want to break away and be independent, and at the same time are highly insecure and attached. They want your guidance and advice and yet will never consider what you advise them to do. They feel an urgent need to live up to tremendous internal and external expectations and thus feel frustrated. In a bid to be viewed as mature, they constantly question or battle with authority figures and each day comes with episodes of ego clashes.

Coping Mechanisms and Maturity

With glandular and physiological changes, teenagers become increasingly uncomfortable with their bodies, secondary sexual characteristics, and sexual orientation. Given all the confusion and frustration, they start emotionally detaching themselves from their parents. Besides, since they are battling numerous insecurities, they become extremely sensitive to criticism as they want to be loved and accepted for who they are.

Most teenagers, unable to cope with this phase, develop unhealthy coping mechanisms and problem-solving abilities. This leads to further confusion in decision-making or healthy life choices. Independent thinking gets affected, thus creating more stress, anxiety, conflict, and confusion. This leads to low frustration tolerance, shame, and guilt.

The Psychology of an Adolescent's Parent

Society is constantly going through a process of change, in terms of attitudes, cultural norms, values and morals. Joint families are disappearing and many more nuclear families are emerging. More parents are educated, working, professionally focused, and career-driven. This leads to less quality family-time. Factors such as single parenting, divorce, death or family discord also contribute to teenage stress.

We, as adults and parents, seem to confuse our teenagers the most. We sometimes have deep subconscious desires that we need our children to fulfil, which build into unrealistic expectations or goals. Our beliefs and sentiments are very often forced upon them, which only make them discredit and disregard us. We lose that respect especially when we do not accept their individuality or give them space and freedom of thought to make their own choices—be it religious beliefs through customs or faith; inter-caste marriages, arranged set-ups or being allowed to find one's own life partner; gender disparity, sexual choices or orientations; career choices and professional paths.

Signs and Symptoms to Look Out For in Teenagers

- Low or swinging moods, sadness, emptiness or irritability most of the day, nearly every day
- Feelings of helplessness, hopelessness or worthlessness and inappropriate guilt
- Lack or loss of interest or pleasure in almost everything
- Negative thoughts and perceptions, recurrent thoughts of death or dying with suicidal ideations
- Academic decline, diminished ability to think, focus, decide, and concentrate
- Refusal to go to school or college, social withdrawal
- Physical symptoms, psychosomatic symptoms such as nausea, stomach aches or headaches, dizziness, back or neck pains
- Fatigue, low energy, changes in appetite and sleeping patterns, with significant weight loss or weight gain
- Psychomotor agitation, restlessness or retardation
- Long periods of time spent locked in the bedroom or bathroom.

Injury marks or cuts on the arms, wrists or upper thigh as self-harm is a way of expressing or dealing with deep distress or emotional pain. It is an unhealthy way of coping. It is a distraction from the emotional pain and perhaps a subconscious way of crying out for help. Look for bandages or band aids which may be frequently used or long-sleeved clothes to constantly cover the injured areas.

Fussy eating habits, eating very sparsely, watching calories or using extreme health diets are other signs. Wasting food or eating extremely small portions, binge eating and then throwing up, constantly weighing oneself or expressing concerns of weight gain when there has been actual weight loss are common. Watch out for odd comments about his/her own body or weight, bruising of skin, hair fall, irregular menstruation, and over-use of laxatives, enemas or diet aids.

What You Need to Do as a Parent

Be your teenager's friend first then a parent, with the mature balance of authority, discipline, and permissiveness.

Step down from your 'parent ego state' and work on the teenager with your 'adult ego state' with rationality and explanation.

Always set a precedence and live by example. Practise as you preach. Never persist on telling them what they have to do and want they cannot do. Allow them to be independent thinkers. Move with the times and connect at their level so they may feel understood.

Set boundaries and systems with consistency and understanding, always giving them reasons and explanations. However, never relent or compromise on certain core family values, beliefs, values, and morals.

Pick the bones of contention with them and always listen to

what they have to say without pre-conceived judgement, bias, criticism or ego. Try and think it through from their perspective, it may make sense !

Never criticize them or their friends in front of others or with family. Never tell on your teenager, especially if he or she has told you something in confidence. They tend to lose faith in you and it takes a while to then win back their trust.

Do not deny a teenager his/her space, privacy, freedom or independence regarding friendships, relationships, phone calls, emails, text messages and so on. That is an invasion for them. They need to be respected.

However, if your intuition or gut tells you that something is not right and it may be a serious matter concerning your child's health or safety, then break down all walls or barriers of privacy to check or find out. Be discreet about this and always give him or her a chance to come clean or open up first.

Talk openly, freely and age-appropriately to your adolescent about the 'difficult stuff' in life too—sex education, dating, relationships, substance abuse, the internet and social media safety, death, divorce and abuse, among other spheres. Do so intelligently, scientifically and sensitively.

When there is an aggressive outburst use time-out and walk away from the situation so that you do not aggravate yourself or the situation. Explaining, arguing or persisting to put forth your point across are futile. Teenagers have an amazing ability to calm themselves down and introspect, especially when the impulsive emotions have passed and they are riddled with guilt.

Seeking professional help is of utmost importance. Consulting a counsellor, psychologist or psychiatrist is essential, but first approach one without your teenager. Permission must be taken from your child if you want a professional to intervene. An explanation must be provided, that the entire family needs guidance and that it would be done in a professional and confidential manner. It is also very important for your child to feel comfortable, safe and secure with the professional that you have chosen. Ample time must be given as well. Open-mindedness towards pharmacotherapy must also be maintained at all times.

Life then comes around a full circle. As your teenager matures and time passes by, you as parents will be slowly seeing yourself in the child you once knew. Sincerity, integrity and loyalty will merge, and a sense of responsibility will replace dependency. You can then heave a sigh of relief and relax for a while in the knowledge that he or she is slowly becoming what you have tried to be or wanted to be or secretly wished to be. If you have achieved bringing up a healthy child in body, mind and spirit, then you know that at some level you have also achieved a higher awareness of yourself...

Chapter 6

MY SIDE

Sexuality, Abuse and Anxiety

'To be fully seen by somebody, then, and be loved anyhow...
this is a human offering that can border on miraculous...'
—Elizabeth Gilbert

Hello Mom,
I have wanted to write to you and communicate my feelings
for a while now, but never got down to actually sending this
letter to you. I kept it saved for over a year but I need to say
this and life is too short. I have gone over this in my own
head now a hundred times. I have had this conversation
with you in my imagination a thousand times. I have
thought over your reactions and what you would say in
response a million times and it is all so predictable. With the
strain between us, I fear you may think less of me at the end
of this. But I am taking my chances as I know that you love
me. You may not understand where I am coming from or
you may not accept or respect me, but I do love you and hope
that one day you will come to appreciate my position.

You have been a strong mother. You have courageously
gone through a traumatic marriage, bringing us up like a
single parent. You have worked hard to provide the best for
us and given us good lines. You have been over-protective
and fiercely dominating in your opinions and thoughts,
sometimes unbearable! You have been rigid, stubborn,
inflexible and obsessive but, all in all, a great mom.

However, you were fighting for so much throughout your life that you stopped noticing me. You were so desperate for the situation at home and for us to be 'perfect' that you made no allowances for shortcomings. You became selfish in your thoughts and beliefs, leaving no place in your head to consider what was actually happening. Or did you choose not to consider it? I will never know.

That is when I realized I had to find a way out or I would get stuck like you, become like you, think like you and you would be making all the decisions for me in my life. You have never been able to accept me for who I am. And I haven't been able to accept myself either, until this juncture. Thus I can be true to my feelings now and share them with confidence and deeper understanding.

It all began in school. I never felt like the other boys in my class and I never knew why. I hated football but loved watching ballet. My mannerisms, my voice, the way I walked and sometimes my gestures were feminine. (In time I would consciously try to mask these characteristics and trained myself to observe and emulate other boys and men.) I would secretly try on your make-up or wear your clothes just for fun and enjoyed it immensely. I started getting extremely close, possessive and obsessive about my 'best friends', and felt devastated if we fell out. I would go into depression after fights or misunderstandings and had very high expectations of them.

I went through a horrible time in school in my senior classes. Boys would ridicule and tease me. I was called a faggot, eunuch, gay bastard and other filthier names constantly. The girls in class who I was close to drifted away and did not want to be associated with me anymore as most of them were dating those boys. That made me feel even more jealous and envious. I did not even understand why all this was happening.

In class ten, when you and Dad were having the worst fights, Sam Uncle used to come down from London during our summer vacation and stay with us for two months. This happened for a couple of years. As we stayed in our older flat with just two bedrooms, he shared our bed at night. Kyra was only seven years old and I was fifteen. Sam Uncle was thirty-five years old then.

I don't even know how to say this, Mom, but after we all went to bed, Sam Uncle would hug me, touch me and then make me touch him. For days I would pretend that I was asleep, my heart pounding, frightened as hell of being caught, feeling guilty, ashamed, disgusted and yet perversely enjoying it as it became more regular. Initially, when I would push him off he would make me feel horrible the next day. Ignore me, purposely pay Kyra more attention, not talk to me and not even look at me for a few days at a stretch. I once remember that he did this to me for an entire week and I felt so frustrated that I initiated the next move. I took his hand, I made him touch me and I kissed him for the first time.

I remember being awake the entire night and then vomiting early the next morning. I thought of myself as the filthiest person ever. Guilt had become like my second nature and I lost all my self-confidence. He was thirty-five years old and I was fifteen. I was a child, Mom. Why wasn't anyone there to see what was happening, to protect me or to help me?

I remember that sometimes days before he was to arrive, I would beg and plead with you to make him sleep separately. You then yelled at me and said that I was spoiled and fussy! What made me really ill was that I think I fell in love with him. I could not get him out of my head. His face, his body, his hair, his smell. Obviously, in a few years he stopped visiting and he must have forgotten about me and thought that I had forgotten him. How could I?

What I had mastered though was the art of suppression. Any feelings, thoughts and memories I had, I pushed deep down into the depths of my mind. At times I forgot what reality was and what may have been a fantasy or imagined. Years later, I even questioned whether things really happened between Sam and me or was it my own imagination?

My suppression and subsequent metamorphosis was like a miracle. Even you stopped ridiculing me. Otherwise, ever so often, I was told off by you—you'd urge me to behave more like a man, stop being a girl; you never allowed me to cry and always said my hypersensitivity was my greatest weakness. You cared a great deal about what people and society would think. Your friends had become far more important to you than your family.

Moreover, your husband, my dad, had consumed you with all your hatred, anger, and emotions. You had made it your mission by then to take revenge on him, make his life miserable and in the bargain, affect all our lives. Thank God he died a few years later. The saddest truth was that I was almost relieved in college when he was no more. You never allowed us to love him. You never allowed him to be our father. I know he cheated on you, Mom, perhaps several times, but there were other ways of expressing your disappointment and anger. Other ways of fighting, coping or dealing with the situation. You damaged our entire childhood and early family life in your fight. Like I mentioned, you stopped noticing everybody else around you. I was sexually abused, Mom, for years and you never knew.

I never blamed you and don't wish to either. I just want

to share facts and the truth, and want you to be aware of the situation. Things did happen besides you, Mom.

So like I said, I changed and was mighty proud of myself. I could mask feelings, emotions and thoughts so well that I almost forgot who I was. I even had a few girlfriends in college but nothing lasted. Every time I fantasized I still thought of Sam Uncle. This was my shame, my guilt, my fault. This is when I started sliding into major depression and even thought of committing suicide a couple of times. I couldn't come to terms with who I actually was.

That's when I started meeting Reshad, my psychologist, who made me understand what had happened in a different light and gave my life another direction; he gave my thoughts another perspective. I wish you had seen him professionally too, Mom, to understand me better. You ridiculed me then too and scoffed at the idea of visiting a shrink, calling it a waste of time and money.

I chose to move out of the house. I planned my educational path so that I could move to London. This had nothing to do with Sam.

Reshad also made me realize that Sam had hugely influenced my life and that what he did was wrong. But he was not responsible for my sexuality. Yes, Mom, that is what I have been trying to say for so many years, in a hundred different ways, especially when you still lament that I need to find a wife. I do not blame Sam for my sexuality. I now no more blame you or myself. I just wish that you would accept me for who I truly am and what I believe in. I have been through hell and into dark places you cannot imagine. I have been through severe bouts of anxiety and panic attacks, knowing that I may never have a life partner, a wife, children or a family to be with me when I am old or dying. I would always be part of a group that is still shunned, ostracized and looked down upon.

I just want us to start afresh. I want you to be my best friend. I crave sharing my innermost feelings with you and wish to be heard. I pray that you understand, accept, and respect me unconditionally. I need you to know that I do not have a medical condition or a psychological disorder that should be treated. In the past, horrible treatments were given to homosexuals, like strong medications with severe side-effects, electro-convulsive therapies and other inhuman experimental measures. My sexuality is a preference, a choice that I have now made. I am not ready to tell the world. I am yet to come out to most of my friends. But feeling accepted and understood by you first means everything to me. I hope that you find a place in your heart to extend some consideration and grant me closure.

You must promise me that you will never speak to anyone about what is to come. I met Sam in London last week, Mom. It took some courage and inner strength to confront him. I spent a long time with him at his home. He is the loneliest fifty-five-year-old man I know. He shared that he was going through major depression and that he was taking medication. He is unemployed. He reminded me of all my fears and the place I don't want to be in. He reminded me of all my nightmares for the future. I could never wish such solitude on my worst enemy. Before I left he hugged me, broke down and wept bitterly for a few seconds. I had already forgiven him but never uttered a word. I will never meet him or see him again for the rest of my life.

So this has been my journey, Mom. I think I have said enough. This outpouring is in no way meant to hurt you and if I have, I apologize from the depths of my heart. I reiterate—you have been and always will be the greatest mom in the world. I am proud to be your son. I love you unconditionally and only hope that you wish to see me happy.

Yours always,

Jehan

*

Jehan's sister Kyra became even closer to him after he came out of the closet. But his mother never replied to his email or called. She stopped taking all his calls. Jehan's therapist, Reshad, too tried reaching out and writing to her but to no avail. Through few friends and family members she made it very clear that she would not meet Jehan when he returned for his breaks from London. She openly commented that she was disgusted with his way of life and was deeply hurt by all his accusations and assumptions. She even blamed his psychologist for not treating him correctly. She blamed Jehan for being a bad son and abandoning her when she needed him the most. She insinuated that he had become delusional and wrongly accused close family members of wrongdoing—all figments of his filthy mind. Against Jehan's wishes, she called and confronted Sam who vehemently denied everything.

Jehan's mother passed away two and a half years after he sent his email. They never spoke, they never met…

The Psychology Guiding Sexuality

Sexuality is part of what makes us human. It is a fundamental, innate function, as is the need to procreate and propagate the species.

However, sexuality is a hugely complex term, and various factors contribute to one's orientation. What Freud termed as 'id', and later described as part of the psychosexual stages of development and also while analysing the controversial Oedipal phase; what Jung called the 'shadow'—the anima or animus, play a major role in sexual attraction.

The development of sexuality is an integral part of the development in children. A range of emotional, psychological, and experimental sexual activities develop before or during early puberty. Child sexuality is influenced by cultural, social and peer-related experiences, behaviours and familial factors or influences. This manifests itself in the form of deep curiosity about the human body, nakedness or private parts. Children also quickly discover as young as the age of five or six that touching certain body parts feels good. At this stage they are also consciously aware of the differences between boys and girls and are more social in their exploration. In their innocence, certain masturbatory behaviours, exploring private parts with other children or following role models of adult behaviour, such as touching or kissing may not be uncommon.

By the age of nine to twelve years, masturbation may begin in private and sexual curiosity increases. Attempts to see people undressing, pictures on the internet or other media may be common. Pre-teens are marked by the beginning of sexual attraction, exploration and a clearer understanding of (or rejection of) morals and social rules. At this point, sexual behaviour tends to be impulsive, unplanned and voluntary between two pre-teens or teens of around the same age, who regularly meet each other.

At this stage or after, many adults recall having a strong affiliation with or sometimes attraction to the same sex in school, but usually they suppress such feelings, thoughts or urges, deeming them as culturally or socially inappropriate. Studies now quite clearly indicate that one is born with a certain orientation. Most old theories about parenting and nurturing contributing to homosexuality are now redundant.

When a child's family rejects their offspring's sexuality, the odds of attempted suicide are nine times higher. Gay youths try to take their own lives four times as often as their heterosexual peers.

What Parents Need to Do to Foster a Healthy Sexual Attitude

If we hope as parents that our children will be global citizens one day, then very early on in their lives, we need to instil the basic values of acceptance and tolerance.

And such values begin with us, and our approach. We need to lead by example at home and in our schools and as parents and teachers act as role models. Children are like clean slates—transparent, honest and innocent—upon which we imprint our behaviour and belief systems.

The stigmas, aversions and preconceived notions children display stem from us. Similarly, the openness and faith kids exhibit are also linked to our value systems. Our worldview percolates subconsciously from generation to generation, family to family. Thus we need to mask and control our own thoughts, behaviour or actions, especially when around our kids.

We need to treat people with respect and be consistent in our attempts at 'niceness'. Irrespective of gender, caste, creed, religion, skin colour, culture, socio-economic status, family background or sexual preference, people should be accepted for what they are. Equally, we need to remind our children how not to discriminate on the basis of these external factors.

All schools and educational set-ups need to have mandatory talks, sessions or workshops for students and parents regarding fraught topics like sexuality, to create more insightful awareness and initiate new independent thought processes in children, so that they may be more accepting.

How to Disconnect Anxiety from Sexuality, as a Parent

Always be alert, aware, hands-on and consciously observant of what is happening at all times in your child's life. To achieve this, keep the channels of communication open between you and your child.

Instil honesty and transparency irrespective of what you are sharing; but it has to work both ways.

Ensure there is constant supervision wherever your child may be, and safety when and where he or she sleeps, well into their teenage lives.

Always believe in your child and develop sustainable trust at a very early stage, knowing that he or she will be comfortable talking to you about anything.

Do not display any discomfort when asked adult-like questions. Answer age-appropriately and as clinically matter-of-fact as possible. Provide relevant educational information that is appropriate to the child's age, social development, understanding and maturity levels.

Ensure you give the child relevant information and provide rules and boundaries regarding personal space, private parts, good touch and bad touch, physiological functions and the anatomy of body parts at a very early age, that is, around five to six years of age.

Stay calm and do not react impulsively when any worrisome situation or behaviour occurs. Your child will only recoil further and shut down communication.

Teaching him or her about abuse, being strong and saying 'no', always sharing an incident no matter with whom, especially if the perpetrator is known to the child and how it is never his/

her fault. This is of primal importance especially in the age groups of six to twelve. A very high percentage of abusers are known to the children they target.

Some rules about safety when using social media and networks, pornography, photographs, dating, masturbation, early pregnancies, sexually transmitted diseases, and HIV are necessary through sex education.

When Your Child Comes Out...

When a child first comes out to his parents, it can be quite a traumatic experience for both the child and parents. Most initial responses seemingly come out wrong. At first, parents may feel hurt because they may be the last ones to know about the child's orientation and are riddled with shock, disbelief, denial or panic. Most parents internalize thoughts on how to 'change' their child.

Counselling ensures coming out becomes a family issue and facilitates insights with healthy and transparent communication. Parents need to understand that it is most important for their children to feel accepted by them first, because they are loved the most. Ridiculing them; telling them that it is perhaps a passing phase; threatening them to change; telling them that it's against religious beliefs; forcing them to see prospective spouses for the purpose of an arranged marriage, blaming it on their peers or bad company or taking them perforce for 'treatment' as if their sexual orientations were diseases, are the things parents must *never* ever do. This can be harmful and psychologically very damaging to the child.

Parents may have these responses because they feel terribly guilty. They perhaps intuitively knew deep down that something was not right, but did not do anything about it. They either blame themselves or their spouse. Some theories suggest a passive father figure or a dominant mother, but these are only theories. Some parents may feel tremendous grief that their child will never marry and have children. They feel their family tree would be cut short. They need a professional explanation to learn that sexuality has nothing at all to do with 'parenting'. Scientific research has clearly indicated biological and neurological factors.

Parents need to start by listening to their children so that there may be a sense of recognition and acceptance. This will make the child more comfortable to express himself and not feel exposed, hurt and anxious, or judged.

Parents need to be gentle and calm and say nothing that is impulsive or irrational. Each word or reaction at this stage is crucial and leaves an impression. This helps the child get less confused and be more honest with his feelings and loved ones.

Help the child talk openly about sexual orientation to very close friends and family members, always taking his permission first. He needs to hear that he is loved and respected irrespective of his orientation.

After there is true inner acceptance and understanding of the situation, it is very important for your child to know that you are proud of him. Guiding him in difficult situations with peers or at work; defending him when he is hurt and being sensitive to his feeling go a long way in the parent—child bonding. Being evolved as a parent is also accepting and encouraging him to find a partner or including his partner in family gatherings or outings.

Sexual Abuse

Child sexual abuse is widely regarded as a cause of mental health problems in young adult life. It affects the child's developing capacity for trust, intimacy and sexuality. It leads to behavioural and conduct issues, impacting school life and academic functioning. It may impact social, sexual or inter-personal functioning in future adult life. Various symptoms may lead to post-traumatic stress disorders, anxiety and depression, issues with self-confidence and self-esteem, alcohol or drug abuse. There is also a future risk of the child developing a tendency to behaviour like domestic violence, poor family attachments, marital discord and abuse in his own future adult life. Issues with intimacy and reduced sexual esteem have also been found in victims.

I would like to point out that not all incidents of child abuse or homosexual molestation define sexual preference in the victims. As for the perpetrators of this crime—it's important to bear in mind that many child molesters do not really have an adult sexual orientation. They may have never really developed the capacity for mature, meaningful sexual relationships with other adults. Some perpetrators are so repressed, regressed or suppressed in their need for expression that children, unfortunately, become easy targets.

Signs and Symptoms of Sexual Abuse to Look Out For

- Any display of behaviours beyond the child's developmental stage, which is not age-appropriate—in relation to another child or an adult (which may include children of widely different age groups; a parent or teacher).
- Sexual behaviour beyond harmless curiosity which is repetitive, forceful or aggressive. Behaviours that mimic or role play adult sexual behaviours or heightened sexual curiosity.
- Manifestation of other behavioural or psychological symptoms of anxiety, social withdrawal, fears, academic decline, loss of attention, concentration or focus, self-

stimulatory behaviours or refusal to attend school, among others.

- Infections, reddening, bruising or itching of private parts.

A Healing Touch

Healing your child recovering from sexual abuse is of primal importance and parents play a very crucial role in this phase. The child needs ongoing support, belief and protection to help overcome any guilty feeling. The most important message needed is that the child is not to blame for the abuse. Parents also need ongoing support, counselling and guidance in every step of the way to ensure they are on the right path in helping their child.

Initially, it is very important to spend lots of quantitative and qualitative time with your children, even if it means taking time out from work. This gives them a sense of security and comfort. However, spending time should be done tactfully, always ensuring a 'normalized' environment at home. No matter how deeply disturbed or saddened you may be as a parent, mask your feelings because they may feel they have done something wrong to bring about this mood, which may compound their guilt.

Accept certain 'acting out' behaviours; however, do not compromise on discipline. Always explain and reassure that you understand why your child may be upset, angry or sad. Help him find healthier coping mechanisms to vent his anger. Let him feel that he can openly discuss matters or the incidents on his mind freely with you without feeling awkward, disturbed or ashamed. This is a good beginning. One must also encourage the child to be honest and open with his counsellor. There may be many details that he would keep from you for obvious reasons, but feel comfortable enough to express the same to his therapist. Do not feel guilty or upset if this happens—it is healthy and needs to be respected.

Always let your child know that you have always believed in and trusted him. Reassure him that he should never blame himself and that he will be completely safe and secure from here on. Let him feel that you are proud of him whenever he shares confidential information. Let the child choose which parent to share that comfort with. Sometimes children get upset if they feel one parent is sharing his concerns with the other and may stop communicating. Give him ample space and never pressurize him to open up or talk.

Never let your child feel that you blame yourself for the abuse or that you have become cynical, bitter, angry or revengeful. This will make him confused and lead to seeing these negative emotions or behaviours as models to follow. Often, we tell our children to try and forget everything that has happened. This will only lead to them using suppression as a defence mechanism, which is very detrimental to the healing process. Problems may then surface in their adult lives.

Support groups or talking to other parents whose children have been abused is very useful as it helps to take suggestions and advice from people who can truly empathize with the situation. Remember you have to be extremely strong and psychologically healthy in order to help your child get by the traumatic experience with confidence, security, and strength.

Never fear that disclosing or exposing will disrupt the family, especially if the perpetrator is a family member or friend. This will add to the child's guilt. The message cannot be ambivalent. What is wrong is wrong and it has to be punished. Reporting, using legal guidance and help from judiciary systems is strongly advised. This provides the family with some closure.

Some children who disclose sexual abuse may take back the admission. This is known as recantation, a common reaction as they may have confused or mixed feelings towards their abuser, especially if the offender is known to the child. This may also happen if the child has been sworn to secrecy or has been threatened in any way. Accepting the abuse is extremely difficult in situations like these. The saddest part is that in some families the child is pressured to recant for various reasons such as society or family pressures, what people will think, fears that no one will marry the child later or in some rare cases, if the parent is the perpetrator itself. Sometimes long legal procedures may also dishearten the child, thus making him recant. In very few cases children may do this because they have made a false statement or wrongly accused someone. This, too, needs intensive counselling to understand why the child did so.

It is mandatory for schools and homes to employ prevention strategies and safety measures. Children who have been subjected to abuse and their families, need intensive professional psychological and psychiatric intervention with therapy and counselling.

Chapter 7

DEAR DOCTOR

Death, Bereavement and Depression

'You would know the secret of death. But how shall you find
it unless you seek it in the heart of life...'
—Kahlil Gibran

Dear Doctor,
I write this because you said it would help me to reflect on
all my feelings and would be therapeutic. You also said it
would help you to understand me better. So here it goes. I
have weeks and pages to fill so I don't know where to begin
and how this will go.

I spoke about my experiences for the first time in our last
two sessions. It felt good and at the same time it made me
feel worse. I guess reliving past memories and pain, and
going through hurtful visuals in my head again and again
distressed me. I don't know if I will ever feel happy or live in
peace again. Yet, I need to, I have to.

The horrible memories started way back when I was
eleven years old. I was in class six at school and used to dread
coming home. After getting off the school bus, my feet would
feel heavy and I would purposely walk as slowly as I could,
to delay reaching home. I would enter the elevator, press No.
9, our floor number, and feel the lift go up while my heart
would sink down. Mum would be in a horrible mood for
most parts of the day. She would seem disconnected and low

all the time. She was angry and upset with Dad mostly. They had been fighting a lot. They always thought I was too young to understand what was going on and most times they even stopped pretending in front of me that things were fine between them. The abuses became worse and the screaming louder. They yelled more than they actually spoke to one another. I would press my ear hard against their shut bedroom door to hear what they were fighting about, but I never quite understood the reasons. I just remember feeling the immense hatred they had for each other.

I stopped existing for them. I remember once when our maid was on leave and their fight in the bedroom never ended, I forgot to eat. They did not even realize it until it was past 11 p.m. and I had gone off to sleep by then.

Sometimes, both tried their best to pretend the situation was normal. They would attempt to smile, or strike a conversation or ask me a whole lot of questions. They would suddenly realize that I had homework or a test to prepare for, and then back off from each other.

It was lonely at home. Initially, I remember the fear gripping me to a point where I would feel nauseous with the emotion. I could not eat, would start sweating and sometimes even lock myself in the bathroom for over an hour until I could hear silence. The fear slowly ebbed away, giving way to anger tinged with constant anxiety and worry.

The feelings that were worse, however, were of isolation and being completely alone. There was no one I could share all the details with as I was embarrassed and ashamed of my parents' ugly fights. If I attempted to talk to my grandmom about it, my dad would get extremely mad at me and her for interfering. I could never tell my friends as they wouldn't understand and afraid that they would tell others, I could *never trust them. When I once asked a friend whether his parents fought, he told a few kids in class that my parents were getting a divorce. Three kids in my class had parents who were separated. They looked different. They had a lost look in their eyes, barely laughed or joked. Kids always whispered about them and my biggest fear was ending up like them. There was always the million dollar question hanging over these three kids' birthday parties. Will the father come? Will the mother's new husband be there? Does the father have a younger girlfriend now? The gossip and speculations were endless. And this went on for years. Deep down the most anxiety-provoking question always lingered, will they get divorced?*

As years went by, I thought my dad was the nasty one. To me it seemed he had a filthy temper, was obsessive and a perfectionist by nature. Things had to be his way. He would say the meanest of things to my mom and increasingly, in front of me which I disliked the most. But the worst was when they fought in front of the domestic help. Mom had no self-respect left when that happened. One would think that after so many years her tears would dry up, but not my mom's. For me she was too soft, gentle, and sensitive.

Towards the end of my class nine, Mom changed. She and I became really close and she started sharing a few things with me—sometimes about Dad and their fights, but she never complained about him or said anything against him. I respected her for that. She, in time became more like a friend to me, and we became really close. She was for me the best mom in the whole world. We shared secrets, we would shop together, she pampered me and made me feel special. By then she had virtually moved into my bedroom. She would snuggle into bed with me late at night, mostly after their fights. I could feel her shake sometimes, either in fear or because she was silently sobbing.

However, even when we were together, without Dad, she always looked very sad. Her smile was melancholic. The best sound in the world to me was when she occasionally laughed, which was very rare. I would cherish that sound and try to recall how it sounded when the gaps became too long.

At some point through my crazy class ten year, preparing for my board exams became really hard. Dad did not even back off, even though he knew that I needed peace in order to concentrate. That year I think I grew up overnight. It was the first time I saw bruises on mom's hand. That was also the first time I asked her what was going on and why Dad was hurting her. I also asked whether separating would be a better option. All she said, despairingly, was 'Where can we go?'...I will never forget the helplessness in her voice. I started hating my dad then. I could not bring myself to speak to him. I was afraid and embarrassed.

As a few more years passed, Mom and Dad began going to doctors. At that time I did not realize that they were going for counselling, something I found out much later. Their relationship seemed far more cordial and quiet, and Mom slid into a phase of silence for most days.

I got really busy with college and friends. I knew I had to start having my own life, and create my own distractions and happiness. I even started dating a boy who is still very much part of my life today. I tried to keep myself away from home as much as I could. I made up stories of birthday parties, overnight plans, three-day projects at my friends' houses, homework assignments until late at night and so on. No one at home asked questions so I took advantage of this.

I started enjoying my life and even decided a career path in psychology. I loved the subject and found my studies meaningful. I wanted to help people and other families, I guess. I was on a high and then one fine day I will never forget, there was Dad's voice on my mobile phone, asking me to come home immediately.

My mother had committed suicide…At that time I was nineteen years old. She had swallowed a few of her prescription tablets and then flung herself out of the bedroom window.

After getting out of the car, my feet felt heavy as I entered the apartment. I was in a daze. All I remember was Dad's face. He was in shock, defeated and appeared broken. He tried to hug me, but I pushed him away with all my strength and shut myself in the bathroom. I wanted to jump off too. I wanted my mother. I wanted to follow her. There were so many things unfinished, unsaid and undone. I could not remember the last time I said 'I love you' to her. I wanted to hear her again, not just remember the silence. Why had she done this to me? Why had she left me alone? Why had Dad done this to her? What would happen now? How could I ever forgive Dad ? Where would I even begin picking up the pieces?

What haunts me the most are memories of the next two days. I will never forget the blood-soaked crumpled body or the horrible thick scar and stitches of the autopsy from her neck going all the way down across her body. I will never forget the scent of death. Nor the crackling sounds of the pyre during the funeral. Letting her go through the cremation door was the hardest thing ever. The last time I would be able to see or touch her.

Those memories did not leave me. It has been eight

months now since Mom's passing and I haven't been able to heal. I have not been able to get back to college. I barely step out of my home or meet my friends. I feel terribly guilty if I do. I hate dressing up because I remember her smiling in delight whenever I did and she would tell me how beautiful I looked. I hate looking at the sun setting from my window as every third day or so she would call out to me if I was home to see how beautiful the sunset was. Sometimes I would just pretend or lie to her that I had already seen it. The guilt of lying to her on so many occasions is eating me up from within.

I cannot bring myself to eat specific food items which were her favourites. I cannot bear anyone laughing like she did. It fills me with rage if anyone does so especially in the house. I cannot sleep in the same bed that we used to share as I start weeping uncontrollably, so I spend many nights on the floor. I can still smell her on the pillow cases and bedsheets which I haven't allowed anyone to wash. I am afraid I will forget how she smelled.

The other day I found a few strands of her hair on her brush, which I placed carefully in an envelope. I love opening her cupboard and going through all her personal belongings which I have never done before. It makes me feel close to her. I have been desperately trying to find all the birthday cards or letters which she had ever given to me. I want to preserve everything that she had touched in her life.

I feel guilty if I watch TV or even if something makes me smile. I feel I am completely losing my mind and I am not coping with this loss in a healthy manner. I can understand and rationalize all of this and know that what I am doing is pathological, but I cannot help myself. I feel extremely overwhelmed, depressed and stuck.

What kills me is that I, as a student of psychology, did not see any warning signs of my mother being suicidal. How could I have been so stupid and blind? That is the reason why I cannot study further as I feel completely inadequate. How can I help others if I couldn't help my own mom? I wish I could have saved her. I wish I was at home that day. I wish I had not become so selfish. I wish my dad had died. I wish I had died.

A month passed. My dad and I were home alone one night when I found him seated on Mom's side of the bed, weeping uncontrollably. In a moment of anger, I lashed out and asked him what he was crying about. I said that he had killed her, so he should be happy. I will never forget the look of shock and disbelief on his face.

Later that night, he reached out to me and began talking. What he said actually ripped out my heart. He said that Mom had been suffering from depression for years and had been diagnosed with bipolar disorder. That is why they had so many irrational fights as Mom would keep accusing Dad of having affairs. She was always suspicious and paranoid about his whereabouts and colleagues at work. In her last fight with him, she screamed that he was preparing for a divorce and was going to marry his secretary. My father lamented that he never had a peaceful or normal life. He never shared all this with me because he said that he did not want to turn me against my mother. He also thought that when I was younger, I would not have understood the situation. He also knew that Mom never spoke against him to me. He said I was the best thing for her and her peace of mind. And then he wept bitterly that despite all the treatment, she never felt better. She was never happy. Nothing interested her. She had no joys in life. His guilt, unhappiness, and sense of loss were greater than mine. She had left us both. What my father must have gone through, God only knows.

How am I supposed to get over this? In our second session, you mentioned the need to see some light through the darkness. I can see now what you meant. I never knew my dad. I never thought of him or for him. I lived my entire childhood with a false perception of him. This has worsened my guilt but I do know I can and should make amends. I have started slowly. That night, when he told me about Mom, I let him hold me. I know he has yearned for me, craved for a daughter which I have never been to him. How was I to know all of this? I was only a child then. I still feel I have not grown up enough to deal with it, yet I know I have to. I know he will and has forgiven me.

Now, I have to forgive myself. I have to start living and loving my life once again.

Please help me overcome this loss. I do not have the strength any more. I am emotionally drained and need to find a solution and healthier coping mechanisms.

I want to be able to have beautiful memories of Mom and not nightmares or images that haunt me. I want to let go of the past. I have to be a daughter once again before it's too late.

A lost girl

*

All children and adults grieve differently. Grieving is a very lonely process. We all have to deal with loss internally and alone. Younger children may become withdrawn and their sorrow manifests itself in a range of ways, from attention-seeking behaviours, to anxiety and somatization, tantrums or depressive symptoms. They may find it hard to focus and concentrate in class or there might be a decline in their academic performance. However, children have amazing resilience and better coping mechanisms than some adults do.

Nothing anybody says or does is going to take away the pain and that gut-wrenching feeling. There is no treatment or path to follow which will hasten the process of healing or soothe distressing memories. There is no right or wrong way of coping. Some need to resume schedules and routines right away and bring back normality into their lives and homes as soon as possible. Some need extended time to accept and deal with the trauma, which may stretch into months.

We should never judge how an individual or child experiences grief. The first reaction to loss, death or the illness of a loved one is usually denial and isolation. It is almost like a defence mechanism that helps to buffer and protect the person from the shock and trauma. This passes and usually leads to anger or blame when the reality sets in. Anger may be directed towards the person who has passed away, other family members, doctors treating them or even the hospitals. There is also resentment of the parent who has departed. This is then followed by bargaining and self-pity. There are hundreds of 'if only...' that play out in the mind. Guilt and regrets make one feel more vulnerable and helpless. This then leads to depression and withdrawal. This period lasts for a while and then slowly phases into an acceptance of the loss.

Sudden loss, accidental deaths or suicide make the coping process very traumatic and painful. On the other hand, sometimes the dignity and grace shown by our dying loved ones make it easier for us to cope.

What a Bereaved Child Needs to Do

As a parent or well-wisher, ask the bereaved child to write down everything beautiful that she can ever remember about the person she has lost—things they did together, jokes or secrets shared, holidays taken, quirky habits of the deceased, favourite movies that they cried through and the meals they had together. As time passes there is an inner fear of losing memories of those who have died. Ask the child to keep a photograph of the one lost by her bedside.

Do not keep all personal items, clothes and other belongings as they were. To enshrine a parent's room is not healthy and will not aid the process of letting go and moving on. Do not get over-attached to 'smells' or obsessively search for 'signs' from your loved one. Both will fade with time. Many coincidences may occur, many evocative smells of perfume, soap, shampoo or bed linen may bring back strong sensations, feelings or memories. Perceive this spiritually if you will but yet clinically, scientifically and practically.

Try and block repetitive thoughts and images of the last few days with your loved one, especially images of the last moments in hospital of suffering or trauma, an accident or suicide. Push away memories of the last rites, funerals or rituals. These were mainly meant to give closure, bring family and friends together and help them turn to faith. May families believe in involving children in these processes; however, it is a very individual choice, depending on other cultural or social factors and the child's age. Forcefully substitute these images with positive ones, happy or funny moments, memorable photographs, videos and talks with family members, friends or other loved ones.

Explain that the child cannot expect best friends or close family members to be by her side for extended periods of time. It is not fair on them as it can be extremely depressing and mentally draining to be around bereaved persons for extended periods of time. It feels very empty and alone when they leave and go back to their happy or normal lives, but that is the reality of the situation. One must have realistic expectations.

Help your child avoid going through months of guilt and regret, what one should have said or not said, over fights or last few nasty words exchanged. Guilt over not having spent enough time with the deceased person or not having said 'I love you' enough is natural and many children have displaced, immature or irrational anger towards their parent who is no more. Let them vent and express, yet always provide rational explanations and support.

A bereaved child does not have to sit at home for weeks, not go out or meet friends, not watch a favourite TV show or eat food she likes or play video games. There is no right or wrong. Point out that no one is watching and no one will judge him or her. We have to be strong for our children. However, one cannot be abnormally normal and tough around your child. It will send him or her a very wrong message and will suppress the stages of normal grief. Cry with your children if you need to. Let them know that they are not alone in grief. Let them know that you too terribly miss the loved ones and you too are angry with the parent for leaving so soon. It is okay to be angry and hurt that the parent will not be there for their child's marriage or for the birth of a grandchild, when it takes place.

Many older children go through severe anxieties regarding the future, worrying about who will take care of the finances, bank work, business, car maintenance, housing bills, other expenditures as well as the health of the surviving parent. Address these concerns as soon as possible, when the time is right.

It is crucial to seek help professionally and go through a few sessions of grief counselling. In these sessions the child can give vent to emotions without guilt, without thinking that it will upset anyone further. Death is a life-altering event. It is a very traumatic experience, very often leading to sleep disturbances, anxiety, panic attacks, depression, loneliness, and isolation. Thus counselling helps with the healing process. It helps accepting the permanent void and emptiness that one feels. It will provide healthier coping mechanisms in regaining normal life and routines.

Help the child to regain inner strength in knowing that when a loss hurts, time is of no consequence.

You will find peace in knowing that your departed parent or spouse lives on in your beautiful children. You may suddenly see, hear or feel things in them that immediately remind you of them. Then will come the realization that life is one great big cycle of events. We all come, we all go. Everything in life is transient and temporary. Your child will also feel great melancholy and sadness, but will also learn that life is beautiful, knowing that it may not last for very long. Nothing lasts forever. Everything dissolves into meaninglessness as does permanence. We leave behind everything—our homes, cupboards, shelves, books, beds, loved ones and eventually, our bodies.

Thus, seize the moment with your children. Let loss inspire them to realize that the time we have is too short. Together with them, change your life, do something different, be hopeful, introspect, reflect, chase your dreams and live each day like it is your last.

Chapter 8

HAPPY BIRTHDAY

Adoption and Single Parenting

'Your children are not your children.
They are the sons and daughters of Life's longing for itself.
They come through you but not from you,
And though they are with you, yet they belong not to you...
For their souls dwell in the house of tomorrow,
Which you cannot visit, not even in your dreams...'
—Kahlil Gibran

Dearest Mom,

I know how much you love letters, so today being your seventieth birthday, I decided to write you one on these lovely letter papers I have preserved for years now. I don't know where to begin as I have so much to say. I needed to write today. My thoughts go racing back in time when I was a child. You gave me my first ever letter when I was nine years old. I still have it safely kept in our favourite box with some of my most precious possessions. You gave it to me the day you told me that I was adopted. I do not recall exactly how I felt then, as I think I may have gone numb for a while. Your letter gave me strength to face many situations that I had to deal with in my growing years. Many puzzling things in the past became clear to me. I then understood why Dad's parents would comment on how different my skin colour was from the family's, or how different the texture of my hair was or my features were. When they would say these things I would spend a long time in front of the bathroom mirror wondering what was different in me.

I will never forget how confused I felt when one of Dad's aunts thought I was the housemaid's daughter! Your expressions were priceless and I love to relate the story with humour to my close friends and family. But back then, I wept for days.

I always wondered why Dad never cuddled or hugged me much. I remember him being aloof and distant. He too looked at me differently. You were so strong when he left, but I broke to bits. I never told you but for years I thought that he went away because of me. I always believed that he went away from us because I was the big mistake. I was so fearful because I thought that we would have to leave our home and stay elsewhere or that I would one day be forced to live with him. There were nights when I would lie awake thinking or worrying. My greatest worry was that something would happen to you.

When I finally mustered the courage to tell Lyla, my best friend then, that I was adopted, the entire class got to know about it the very next day. They all looked at me differently when I entered the classroom that morning. I felt so sick that I threw up. You had to come fetch me from school that afternoon. That was the first time you said that I should feel proud to have been adopted—not ashamed or embarrassed. You also jokingly told me to tell my friends that they should all feel proud of you for being so brave being adopted! How did you do it, Mom? How were you so strong? When Dad left, I never saw you shed a tear. You worked doubly hard at your office and at home. You never forgot to make my lunch and place it carefully wrapped in my school bag. You always *cooked my favourite stuff. You woke up at 5 a.m. for years. You never missed going over my homework with me or helping me complete my crazy assignments or projects. You were there at home in the early evening during my examinations and you slept with me after I switched my lights off way past midnight. You came to school for each open day smiling from ear to ear as my report cards and feedback were always fabulous. During our Annual Day concerts you invariably managed to get front row seats for yourself, and I always saw the tears streaming down while I performed or received a prize on stage. Every summer we went for a holiday with our friends or relatives. They were the most beautiful memories ever, whether it was horse riding in Matheran or trekking in Nainital or white water river rafting in Rishikesh. Towards the end of school I was terribly angry with you because almost all the girls in class would be talking about their holidays in Spain, London or Switzerland. I always dreamt of going to those places. I know you did too.*

I know you had to beg Uncle Naresh for my tuition fees through medical school. It was so embarrassing. When you saw me overhearing the conversation with him over the phone, you turned around and winked at me as though you were pretending to beg. You then put down the phone and told me jokingly how we must fleece him as he had pots of gold and cupboards stashed with cash. I noticed all these things in silence and awe. I had grown up a long while back, Mom. I guess I had to grow up and mature way faster than my peers. I never thought much about my adoption because you never once made me feel anything but completely yours. Even after college when I stupidly decided to go on a mission to find my biological parents, you helped me in every way possible. I could see the sadness in your eyes, the fear and apprehensions. I never apologized for that, Mom, so I do so today. I now realize how much pain I must have caused you. I stopped searching because by chance, during that phase, I happened to find and re-read your letter you had given me when I was nine.

When I was considering marrying Anil and had to meet his parents, I was nervous about letting them know that I was adopted and thought of a hundred different ways of telling them. But at dinner with them, you just suddenly and jokingly mentioned how I hadn't popped out from your uterus and that I was born from your heart. Anil almost choked on his wine! Thank you for that, Mom. I also know that for our small wedding reception, which you wanted to host, you sold your jewellery. I found that out years later!

You never allowed me to feel 'different'. How did you manage that, Mom? You never let me feel the loss of one parent. How did you take the place of both parents? You never once let me feel ugly, even though you have been a stunning-looking woman. You always gave me the best. I owned the best school bag in class, the first girl to get a Swatch watch and had the best birthday parties. How did you not get tired, Mom? I never once heard you complain even after a twelve-hour work shift. You never cribbed or complained. How did you become so selfless? When money matters at some point got really difficult, how were there always my favourite pistachio nuts and Godaiver chocolates in the refrigerator? How did you manage so many things so effortlessly and graciously?

So I was looking at you very closely, Mom. I observed you and learned everything from you. Everything I am today is because of you. You gave me life. You gave me inner beauty *and resilience. You have given me the personality that I possess today and you have given me my profession. You gave me a beautiful wedding and accepted my Anil like he was your own. You gave me wings to fly away.*

You make me want to be a better human being, daughter, wife and mother. Your existence and mere presence give me strength and courage to face any challenge. You have taught me patience, integrity, honesty, and sincerity. You have shown me the meaning of dignity and how to command respect. You have shown me the path to my family and how to live in the present moment, never looking back at the past and with no regrets. You have given me the determination never to feel anxious about the future or worry about situations beyond my control. Most importantly, you have taught me to be the best kind of parent to my two beautiful babies. Thank you. There are no other words that I could think of for all that you have done for me and all that you mean to me. All I can say is that I was truly blessed when you chose me to be part of your life.

How I miss you, Mom. It breaks my heart to live hundreds of miles away from you. I am always thinking of you and wishing you would decide to live with us here in New York. Your grandchildren miss you. Our home is always open to you.

So Mom, here comes the big birthday gift! Anil and I have organized a three-month vacation for you in Europe. The tickets, bookings and documents will reach you shortly. Truly, I have wanted to do this for you for a while now. I know it has always been your dream to travel through all of Europe, so here is your chance.

Lastly, Mom, here's the birthday surprise. This letter is to let you know that you have inspired our lives with such

*unconditional love, that Anil and I have decided to adopt a
beautiful baby girl. Sheena is four months old and needs a
home. This is my tribute to you and I hope I can live up to
everything you have taught me. I love you with all of my
heart. Happy Birthday, darling Mom.*

Hugs and kisses,
Me

Psychology of Adoption

There are many reasons why parents decide to adopt a child. It
could be because of medical issues, infertility, failed IVFs, to
help out a family member, taking the responsibility after loss or
death of the biological parents or just to give a needy child a
home. It is a very personal decision and needs to be taken after
much introspection and thought. It is crucial that both parents
should feel the need to adopt equally. Some parents want to
adopt a child from the same religion, background or community
and also feel that the child should have physical attributes
similar to them. Others choose children from orphanages or
those who may have been abandoned. Some may even choose
children with diverse backgrounds, a disability or from war-
torn, poverty-stricken regions or countries. Parents in such
situations need to be well-informed, guided, counselled and
made aware of all the issues that may come up through the
child's development and growing years.

A common occurrence is that couples have their own children
after they adopt. Some look at this as a blessing, but others start
harbouring very different feelings towards their adopted child.
They start rejecting him/her and cannot seem to accept the
genetically different physical attributes, features, mannerisms,
behaviours or personality traits. Some parents, during
counselling, also express that they wish they had not adopted

the child. Subconscious or conscious comparisons made with the sibling can lead to a discrepancy in parenting styles and behaviour. These psychological manifestations can be extremely devastating for the child's emotional repetition well-being as well as hamper his or her overall social and emotional development. Most children in these situations go through trauma and need psychological intervention.

Insights for parents

Talking about adoption with your child is very important. It needs to be done sensitively and age-appropriately. Feelings about being adopted can influence a child's sense of self-esteem and worth. Adoptive parents are in the constant paradox of helping their children understand what it means to be adopted, knowing that in the process the child may feel confused, rejected, sad or hurt. The most commonly asked question that children ask is, 'Where did I come from?' It is always important to provide a truthful answer.

What do we need to do

In the case of an adopted child in the 1–4 age group:

Parents can tell him/her: 'You were born the same way that every other child in this world is—except, you grew inside the tummy of another woman who was still not ready to be a mummy. We desperately wanted to be parents and when we saw you, we just fell in love. We *had* to have you in our lives. On reaching home for the first time with you, all the relatives and friends were waiting. They had a huge party and celebrated all of that day. You completed the family—without you we were lonely.'

In the case of an adopted child in the 5–11 age group:

By this age children begin to understand and recognize the difficult, complicated and confusing aspects of adoption. They may go through feelings of embarrassment, shame, rejection, and isolation—of being different from other children. They wonder why they have been abandoned or given up by their own mothers. They suddenly feel a sense of rejection and start wondering if there was something wrong with them. They cannot rationalize or understand the reasons why a mother would give up her baby. They may go through a phase of being oppositional and defiant. Bouts of moodiness, anger or sadness are common. If they have a sibling who is the biological child of the adoptive parents, there would be significant strong feelings of rivalry, envy and jealousy. They think that this sibling has more privileges or liberties than them. Most of these feelings are exaggerated or wrongly perceived.

Some children will openly talk about adoption and ask why some mothers need to give up their babies. A parent can then explain what the possible reasons may be: the mother may have been too young and not ready to be a parent; perhaps she had no job or financial stability; or she was too ill to look after a baby.

If the child was from an orphanage, he/she should be honestly told that the biological parents were unknown.

Children need to feel extremely secure in this phase of their lives. Open and honest conversations and communication are important without causing the child any sense of awkwardness or discomfort.

In the case of an adopted child of the 12–18 age group:

At this stage of their lives, children are developing their own identity and discovering their own sense of confidence, self-esteem and self-worth. Some children in this phase feel more insecure as the reality of being adopted sets in. There may come a time when they are seized with an obsessive need to search, locate, find or connect with their biological parents. Many thoughts may crowd the mind; they may fantasize about the day they would meet their parents and wonder how they would respond to them. Would they meet affectionately or as strangers? What explanation would they have for giving away their child? In this phase, children find it very difficult to discuss their feelings with their adoptive parents; therefore it is advisable to seek professional help and counselling for them. They feel torn, confused and guilty since they do not want their adoptive parents to feel betrayed or let down.

Parents at this point must make the effort to resolve these questions. Some parents take their adopted children back to the orphanage, adoption centre or country they came from to provide some closure. Many adopted children are even introduced to their biological parents and given the freedom to contact or meet them. Of course, this resolution is only possible when both sets of parents are in agreement with the arrangement. Helping children express their feelings openly is very rewarding for they feel far more confident and secure. They begin to accept the situation and feel grateful to their adoptive parents.

Then one day they will realize the beauty, strength and selflessness of the life-changing decision and journey that their adoptive parents embarked on. They will eventually realize the truth, and say, 'We could never take our parents for granted...never.'

Chapter 9

FATHERHOOD

Parental Anxiety

'No man can possibly know what life means, what the world means, until he has a child...and then the whole universe changes and nothing will ever again seem exactly as it seemed before...'
—Lafcadio Hearn

Dearest Zayn,

After we grow up and find our life's work, become independent and self-sufficient, other needs come by. One of the most important decisions we make, is the choice of a life partner. Choices that are perfect are rare, but those that turn out to be the right ones need to be cherished and treasured. Being grateful to our partner for bearing with us is always something to think about. Decisions such as these need to be made straight from the heart free, from discriminatory factors that could influence or cloud our judgement, such as caste, creed, religion, physical attributes and so on. I am so happy and proud that you have made that choice so perfectly.

Planning to have a child is another monumental milestone in our lifetimes. Our genes and neuronal wiring are replicated in our offsprings. It is almost a selfish and narcissistic need, an innate, animal-like instinct to create someone we can call our own, can possess completely, and who we can nourish, control, mould, nurture, and love unconditionally. This need is perhaps a manifestation of our insecurity, knowing that nothing is permanent. It is our fear of being alone, not being looked after in times of ill-health, growing old and the finality of death.

Then comes the beauty and magic of the birth of a child. We think that our hearts have limited space and are so consumed by love for our mother, father, siblings, spouse and close family or friends, that there is no more room left. It is amazing how that same heart explodes with new, unbelievable emotions when we see our children. It is warming to know how soon our hearts can expand. It is a surreal feeling when we look down upon someone we have created, who is a part of us—the pride and joy are immense.

At the same time, the mind also explodes with a million scary thoughts. Emotions range from shock, panic, anxiety to apprehension, fear, worry, and concern. It suddenly dawns upon us that we are now parents. We are responsible for another life that we have created and brought into this world. We shall, from here on be responsible for this child for the rest of our lives. There is no turning back from this one! Suddenly, we find ourselves thinking about a job, how to increase our income but reduce our work hours (an impossible mission), how to save and invest better, how to plan for the future, how to balance time in our crazy schedules, how to be healthier, how to make our home safe for the baby (yet keep it looking like the beautiful home we are used to...another impossible mission)—responsibilities sky rocket to unimaginable levels. There is also a sudden instinctive protectiveness that sets in, which will remain forever. Then our heart starts pounding even faster at the thought of perhaps having another child...already!

After this comes the overbearing, almost obsessive thought process of the dream-child concept. We envision a perfect baby, healthy in mind and body. Everything else is meant to be secondary. However, the other demands and expectations get over-powering and stronger as the days pass, especially when all nine months of the pregnancy go smoothly. We expect our infants to look perfect, be supremely proportionate, have perfect skin, hair and eyes, perfectly timed sleeping and eating patterns—with no tantrums, reflux or colic. We envision the child growing up with no behavioural problems, completely lovable, obedient, mouldable, and compliant.

We dream that our children will have the most sociable and amiable personalities, be popular and outgoing and have fabulous manners, social skills and graces. We have thoughts of them sitting quietly in their rooms, engaged in reading books or quietly building their blocks or solving a puzzle. We imagine them with articulate speech and language skills, high intelligence—sailing through with honours, merits and distinctions through school life.

There is also a tendency to over-compensate in parents. We want to provide children with everything we never had in our growing up years. We want them to fulfil and achieve everything we could not. We want them to succeed in attaining every dream we could not reach. We wish to provide them with the best support, education and schools, and find opportunities for them for future jobs and professions.

At the birth of a child, everything changes. Our lives are transformed forever. At the very instant of birth, there is a burst of emotion that cannot be described or written down, as it varies from parent to parent.

I remember being inside with your mom in the delivery room. It was not a very pretty sight, let me warn you. You will in those few hours realize how much crazy strength and resilience women have! Your mom had almost crushed my hand to a pulp and at some moments I felt that I was going to pass out seeing all that pain. The very second you came out, I wanted to reach out and hold you or just touch you. But that doesn't happen. The paediatrician whisked you away, rubbed you down and ensured that you cried and were cleaned.

When any father reaches home after a child is born, he will be in a daze for a couple of weeks, my son. As a father-to-be, know that you will be sleep-deprived, fatigued, dreaming of or imagining all sorts of baby sounds. You will be pretending many a time to be fast asleep as your body will just refuse to move. You will be engaged with diaper changes and will start loathing those diapers, especially after you have calculated how many changes you do and how much you will be spending on them. The house will be a war zone with trays, bowls, cotton balls, baby clothes and wraps, breast pumps, sterilizers, hand sanitizers, baby books, squeaky annoying and irritating little toys that you may find under you while sitting on the sofa, or may accidentally squish under your foot. The bathroom is not yours any more. There will be a baby tub, more squeaky water-squirting bath toys in various animal forms and colours and a shelf full of soap, shampoos and bubble baths.

Your throne, the pot (once yours only) may have a smaller funny version of itself besides it, or a smaller potty seat perched on your seat itself. The bin will be flooded with endless balls of rolled diapers stuffed with poop. The odours are mixed. Some are beautiful nostalgic fragrances of baby powder and soap and the other odour ones I'd rather not mention. But you get used to it all, my son.

What will be most terrifying is your new, hormonal, possessive, impatient, moody, sleep-deprived, volatile wife.

She will want you to be the perfect, involved dad and yet won't allow you to do anything independently. The bath is not done right, the water is too cold, milk bottles have not been rinsed thrice, the diaper has not been tied correctly, the hair hasn't been dried properly or you have not succeeded in putting your little one to sleep on time. After all this, you will still be lectured about how you're not good enough a father. You will never feel good enough for a while. You will always feel judged, watched and monitored.

This will depress you and you may resort to comfort eating (please don't, decades later I'm still trying to lose the flab!) You suddenly feel you don't have a life of your own, no independence. You may detach yourself completely for a while from the entire family. You feel affected because suddenly you are no more the priority. You have been displaced by this little creature that has transformed and changed your beautiful, thoughtful, selfless, sensitive wife. Love has been shared and divided. You will feel ignored.

The key advice here is to put up a brave front, join the gym before you start getting severe backaches caused by carrying the baby, eat healthy and try to get a good night's sleep. Always agree with your wife so that your relationship remains positive. Very importantly, when she is in a receptive mood, do express all that you feel. You will be surprised how fantastic women are at multi-tasking. She will change and start looking at you in the same way again, I promise. It would be selfish to expect your wife to attend to you and treat you in the same way as before. It is no more just about you. It suddenly becomes about them, your wife and child.

*

It is so much more important to be a neurotic, hands-on parent, rather than have your baby brought up by a nanny, maid or other house staff members. With today's risks of a caretaker's manhandling, impatience, roughness, abuse, and perversity you'd rather be safe than sorry. In any case, the times you share with your child are extremely short-lived.

How I miss bathing you, feeding you, changing your clothes, rocking you to sleep in my arms with soft nursery rhymes, holding your hand or placing mine involuntarily over the sharp corner of a dining table. With all the chaos and excitement, there have been beautiful memories— looking down at your sleeping body, while holding your palms; putting my finger under your nose to check whether you are breathing; hearing your first few words, watching the first imbalanced steps, seeing those early uncoordinated dance moves (and predicting you will be the next superstar!) and managing your initial tantrums and melt-downs. So many irreplaceable, touching, hilarious memories.

The truth of the matter is that we men are born lazy . It is because of this laziness that we take it for granted that a wife will take charge of the upbringing. And they do. Thus many men miss out on these few crucial years of fatherhood. You have then missed out on some of the best aspects of bonding. And if you do, don't complain that your baby never comes to you or shows any desire to cuddle with you or sleep with you.

Fatherhood is not easy, neither is it automatic. It entails a lot of hard work, effort and sacrifice to be the kind of parent you want to be. Your mother once told me that I had to decide for myself how I want to carry out my responsibility. I still do not know what kind of parent I have been.

Fatherhood is about understanding the purpose of your life here on earth. It is about forgetting about yourself for a while and thinking way beyond yourself as an individual. It is about being selfless for the rest of your life or at least trying to be. It is about investing quality time and cherishing every little moment that you have with our little ones—after all, as your baby grows you will barely be able to recall these tender, fleeting moments; as your baby matures, you'll see that her dependence on you lasts for only a few years. In no time, all aspects of her functioning will be independent.

Time flies by far too fast. As a father you may barely get twelve to fifteen summer holiday stretches with your child. Take time out from work, spend your well-earned money on travelling to see beautiful places in this world and make each second worthwhile with her. Get to know her, be a friend and get so close to her that you have the security in knowing that you have brought her up to the best of your abilities. The way you feel when she wraps her little arms around you or looks into your eyes when she is half-asleep and utters, I love you, straight from her heart, is something that each father and parent should experience and hold on to.

The moments from then on are endless, Zayn. I still recall the first time my stomach churned when you fell and your knees bled. My hands shook and I felt guilty for not being quick enough with my reflexes to stop you from falling. I still feel that way when things do not go right for you. The sense of elation when you for the first time swam across the breadth of the swimming pool after trying for months on end, will never leave me. Or the way you rode a horse independently or cycled away, without me supporting and running behind you like always. My heart broke the first time you came home and complained of a senior boy bullying and slapping you across your face in the school bus. I wanted to kill him! I barely slept in peace during your examination days. I would do so only after your reading light would go off. I always came into your room afterwards to kiss your head. Driving you to school on those days would also be anxiety-ridden. How I wished I could have taken away some of your stress in those days. I never mentioned this to you before, but I would stand in pain with my ear pressed against your door. Hearing you sob when Shanaya had broken off with you in college after two years of dating made me feel so helpless.

Mum and I paced up and down the house continuously for three days after sending you for your first school camp. When you returned, we behaved as though you had gone away for ages. I also remember feeling a bit sad as you never mentioned once that you had missed us. I silently wept in the bathroom when you bought me an expensive watch with your first earnings. It is and will always be my most prized possession. I wept again the next day after your marriage when I walked in to your empty bedroom and sat on your unruffled bed.

The happiness you have brought into my life is incomparable. You and your sister have completed our lives in every way imaginable. I know you will be a wonderful father to your child and I know she will bring to you all the love and magic that you have given us all these years. I am so proud of the man you have become. You have gone beyond all the expectations that I ever had of you. You have taught me so much in my life. You have been responsible for changing me to a better person and guiding me, in a way, to become a better parent! Thank you for being a beautiful son. Enjoy fatherhood like I do mine.

Love always,
Dad

AFTERWORD
When the Leaf Falls

'Within the core of each of us is the child we once were.
This child constitutes the foundation of what we have become,
who we are, and what we will be...'
—Dr R. Joseph

Maybe trees are just like us parents, and leaves like our offsprings.

Each leaf, like our child, is unique and different. No two leaves are the same. They differ in colour, size, shape and texture. The different types of leaves allow one to recognize the tree they come from. Some leaves grow to protect the tree—they may be sharp or spindle-like, have a bitter unpleasant taste, which keeps harm away. They may even mould and adapt themselves to live harmoniously with other creatures, in turn, working to protect them. In the course of evolution, leaves have adapted in various unusual ways to different or difficult environments. Some have formed waterproof surfaces or even wax to avoid damage by rain. Succulent leaves store large amounts of water, while others may have aromatic oils, poisons or pheromones.

Despite this unique bond between the leaf and tree, the leaves eventually fall off. The tree sends a message to the leaves to let go. Once this message is received, little cells appear at the place where the leaf stem meets the branch. They are called 'abscission cells' .They push the leaf bit by bit, away from the stem, preparing them to fall. Trees are deeply programmed by eons of evolution to ensure that the leaves drop away.

Leaves represent our progeny too. We create them, nurture them, protect them, nourish them, mould them and then eventually prepare them to leave. We strengthen them to be eventually independent so that they may survive in the world on their own. They must be strong in both mind and body to handle and cope with what life has in store for them; they must adapt to any environment so they may always be stable and contented. We must see that they develop and evolve so that one day they may procreate and continue the legacy of our families and genes. As they begin the next chapter in their lives, they in turn will also lend vitality, strength and fortitude to their offsprings.

We do not want our children to leave, but it is necessary that they do. It is our duty to set them afloat. The scar of that pain may always remain. We conceal the sense of loss, loneliness, emptiness and the void. What needs to remain is the sense of pride, peace and faith, knowing that you have created a good human being who is perfect in your eyes. Nothing else matters!

When the leaf falls, it must fall in your presence. You need to be around to empower change when and if needed. The winds may be strong and harsh. They may rip right through your gut and their souls. They may take away the leaf too soon. Always be prepared and wise, introspective, and courageous. Always learn and be positive because everything in life happens for a reason. Change is always constant. Some good, some necessary and some unexpected.

Yet one factor remains untouched and unchangeable and that is the unconditional love every parent must have for their child. That is beyond everything. That will give you the power to effect change from deep within and allow unconditional acceptance of your child. Then and only then will life complete that full cycle.

You will, in many moments, receive the same love from your child. You shall be forgiven. You shall be accepted and completely understood. You shall be regarded with utmost respect. In those epic moments, you will feel a sense of release, freedom, power, elation, accomplishment, closure, completion, sadness, regret or intense peace when the leaf falls.

ACKNOWLEDGEMENTS

This book would not have been possible if it were not for the trust, faith and belief of the hundreds of families and their children who have spent their valuable time with me, for over fifteen years. They taught me what resilience, patience, acceptance, and unconditional love is truly meant to be.

This book is not meant to teach or preach. It hopes to create awareness, understanding and insight, through experiences which have taught me so much of life and in living. It is meant to stimulate thinking and, in turn, generate more questioning and learning.

This book would not exist if it were not for my mother and father who created and moulded every part of who I am today.

This is for my wife, for without her I would not know the meaning of mindful, thoughtful and almost perfect parenting.

To my son, who keeps inspiring me to be a better father, and to my daughter, for whom I want to keep trying to be a better human being—to quote from the *Knights of Pythagoras*:

'A man never stands as tall as when he kneels to help a child.'